the detourist

HOW TO GET OUT OF YOUR OWN WAY, FIND PURPOSE IN UNEXPECTED PLACES, AND TRAVERSE THE PATH TO EFFORTLESS AUTHENTICITY

matthew emmorey

ISBN: 978-1-7344182-9-3

table of contents

the road to permanence part 1/4

---

*"If I speak in the tongues of men and of angels,
but have not love, I am a noisy gong or a clanging cymbal. And if I have
prophetic powers, and understand all mysteries and all knowledge, and if I
have all faith so as to remove mountains, but have not love, I am nothing.
If I give away all I have, and if I deliver up my body to be burned,
but have not love, I gain nothing."*

Apenimon was down to his last dollar. He put some gas in the tank of his Chevy C10. The fuel would have to get him the eighty miles from Ulysses to Dodge City, Kansas, where he was told that labor awaited any man with a work ethic. God knew that Apenimon was eager for work. It was a straight enough shot along country roads, but there were never any guarantees in life. Especially not with his old truck. "Someday, this is going to make a great story," he said to himself.

He was told to be out front of the lumberyard in Dodge City at 8am. At 5:55am, he hung the gas pump in its collar and was on his way.

His old truck was not fast. A little after the 6am hour, the bright lights of another vehicle appeared in his mirrors. They did not pass Apenimon right away. Instead, with an illogical and maniacal anger, they rode up against his bumper honking their horn and flashing their brights. When Apenimon had enough, he pulled over in the long grasses on the shoulder and let them pass. He was worked up, and he had plenty of time before 8am, so he spent a few minutes taking deep breaths to calm himself.

Little did Apenimon know that the night before, lightning had struck the train tracks just outside of a little town called Hickok. The surge of electricity had fried the warning mechanism, so when the train rolled through Hickok that morning, the arm did not come down nor did the lights flash. Had he remained on his course, Apenimon would have been crossing those train tracks at precisely the wrong moment. Even ignorant of this fact, Apenimon said to himself, "Everything happens for a reason."

Back on the road, he had time to spare. He rubbed his forearm muscles as he drove, anticipating a hard day's work. The idea of working up a sweat and a paycheck brought a smile to his face. The man relished in hard labor.

About halfway into his drive, the sun came up. It sat itself on the horizon of the highway, making it difficult for Apenimon to see. As beautiful as it was, it blinded the man from seeing a hunk of blown tire lying in the road. He ran over the hunk of rubber, and it leapt into the underbelly of his truck, wreaking havoc. A *thud*, a *groan*, a *hiss*, and then a *knocking* reached his ears. Power withdrew from his gas pedal, and slowly, *loudly*, his old truck shuddered to a halt on the shoulder. "Drat!" He beat the steering wheel with both hands.

At 7am, he popped the hood and looked helplessly at his engine. He was only 10 miles outside of Dodge City. With some luck, he could hitch a ride into town and still make it to the lumberyard with minutes to spare. After work, he could speak to a mechanic about his abandoned truck. "Everything always works out," Apenimon told himself. And then, with a comforting hand on his Chevy's mirror, he said to the machine, "We'll just have to rely on the kindness of others."

Apenimon realized the sun was not doing him any favors. It was still blinding all the eastward drivers, so while he waited for a car to come, he dragged the blown tire out of the road. Just as he did not see the rubbery landmine, the next few cars passed without seeming to see him. By 7:25am, a good dozen cars had gone by without so much as a second look.

But then, *finally*, a car saw his extended thumb and began to slow. When the driver got near enough for Apenimon to see his face, however, the man's eyes bulged in fear and he sped off. "Drat!" Apenimon thought. He was accustomed to prejudice due to his heritage, but under his present circumstances, it hurt a little worse.

But then Apenimon smelled smoke.

He whipped around to look at his truck. It seemed his tailpipe had gotten hot enough to ignite the dry grasses along the shoulder. A small fire had begun to burn underneath his truck! Thinking fast, he shifted the truck into neutral and pushed it forward onto a patch of gravel. "Drat!"

Once the truck was safe, he turned back to the small fire. It was not so small anymore. It had leapt from the stalks along the shoulder to the grasses in the field adjacent. It spat smoke. Within minutes, if Apenimon did not do something, the entire field would be in flames. He removed the hope of making it to Dodge City from his mind, and ran to search his truck for a tool.

He had no fire extinguisher. He had no carton or jug of water. Instead, he came back with a large blanket. He threw the blanket over the flaming grasses and began stomping on it, hoping the fire would go out before he and the blanket became engulfed in flames. It worked, but the fire was larger than the blanket, so he had to repeat his efforts several times before the flames were still. When at long last the fire was out and he could rest, it was 7:50am. He was not going to make it to work.

Apenimon sat next to the scorched grass amongst scraps of burnt blanket. Sweat from the effort and the heat of the fire had soaked through his shirt. He rested, tired and thirsty, sad and disappointed. "I know you're not trying to keep me down, God," he said, "*but why?*"

As if in response, right then, the man spotted something lying beneath the charred grass. It was metallic and shiny, about the size of a wheel. Upon inspection, he saw it was a steel hatch. With a little bit of effort, he got the mechanism to spin counterclockwise. As it spun, he realized what he had found. It was an old tornado shelter.

Eventually, something within *clicked*, and the hatch would not spin any further. As Apenimon heaved, a perfectly square crease appeared in the dirt, and a doorway into the earth appeared. The morning light illuminated a ladder into the depths of the shelter. With a little self-encouragement, he climbed down.

The room was larger than he expected. It was ten feet square. There was a cot in one corner, a few books, a duffel bag, candles, and a few loose pieces of paper, all coated in dirt. Shelves lined the walls, completely stocked with preserves. Hundreds of cans of food and water decorated the walls of the underground room. Apenimon saw jellies, a dozen different pickled vegetables, and more. He took his time analyzing the jars, but as he did, his mind did not wander far from that large duffel.

When finally he unzipped the bag, his heart leapt. Stuffed to the brim of the bag was gold, silver, and old bank notes. It was a treasure. Perhaps $20,000 worth of precious metals and legal tender. Upon analysis, he saw that the bills were over fifty years old. This shelter had been untouched for a long time.

Apenimon searched for any indication of ownership. He found none. With excitement, he loaded the duffel bag into his truck. He went back for armful after armful of preserves. When he was finished, the sun was overhead. It was 11:11am.

But despite the fact that the stores were now completely loaded into his truck, Apenimon did not feel like a rich man. It was never his intention to rob the tornado shelter and make off with the loot. His parents had named him Apenimon because it meant *Worthy of Trust*, and the man intended to live up to his name. He had been blessed with a sign.

Despite the delays, the broken down truck, the fire, his missing work, his being in the middle of nowhere without a dollar to his name, he was exactly where he was supposed to be. This, to Apenimon, above all else, was clear.

So, Apenimon waited happily until a car stopped for him. He asked the driver to send a tow truck from Dodge City. Eventually, his tow arrived and his Chevy C10 was delivered to a mechanic.

Apenimon allowed himself a jar of pickled okra. One jar could not hurt. He asked around the city until he found out who it was that owned that plot of land 10 miles out in the country. The name he received was attached to a well-to-do family. One of them happened to live in town, so while he waited for his truck to be repaired, he walked to the address he was given, snacking on delicious okra all the way.

At the house, he was greeted by a kind woman with a compassionate smile. As Apenimon recounted his story, the woman's eyes kept darting down to that jar of okra. Eventually, once he was finished, she asked, "May I?"

"Of course," Apenimon said, suddenly embarrassed. He offered her the jar. "They belong to you, after all."

The woman's face glowed as she took a bite, as if recalling a fond memory. "Come on inside," she said. "I want you to meet my husband. I have always told him about my grandmother's pickled okra recipe. He will be delighted he gets to try it for himself. And I would very much like you to meet him."

Her husband greeted Apenimon with a firm, sawdusty handshake. The woman insisted that Apenimon recount the tale for her husband. When he was finished, the man said, "You came to town looking for work at the lumberyard? Well, I own the lumberyard, and I am always looking to hire honest men."

at the end of my rope

Wilderness explorers teach that you are not lost until you have no way to get back to *any* familiar location. More often, then, we are not lost but temporarily displaced. The moment you realize your displacement, wisdom says to return to familiarity. Go back to the *Path*. Retrace your steps to where you went astray.

Doubling back, unfortunately, has never been my strategy. I can barely tolerate an out-and-back hike. A loop trail has twice as much mystery. Countless times I have found myself at the critical point between displacement and lost, and chosen to bury myself deeper into the unknown. *I will figure it out.* Hours later, one misstep from falling into a murky swamp, tiptoeing across a dilapidated bridge reduced to rotting boards and crumbling iron, reason finally catches up to me on the trail.

As often as my stubbornness has led to misadventure in nature, it has led to sorrow in life. The natural paths I have wandered off of have led to encounters with bears, cliffs, deep snow, and other hazards, but for the most part, I always knew what I was choosing.

The spiritual wilderness is a different kind of unforgiving. Throughout my life, I have been just as consistent wandering off of this Path as I have the natural others.

The spiritual Path is uniquely yours. It is not laid out with nice stones, nor is it beaten back by previous travelers. It is not clear. It is not well-trodden. It forks off with every footfall, so that constantly, diligently, you must ask yourself, "*What path am I on?*" If one follows the spiritual Path, the one Jesus embodied, they will find their way to a glorious Kingdom. The Kingdom is in full bloom, with cascading falls, lush valleys, symbiotic wildlife, and boundless love, where nothing toils or spins, but all life reaches its head toward the sky to bask in enlightenment.

Calling it a Kingdom will ring in the ears of the saved like music. Unfortunately, it can be nothing more than drivel to the uninitiated. The Kingdom is not a religious place - it is a *sanctified* one.

Jesus said, "I am the way, the truth, and the life."

If one is seeking the Kingdom, He instructs seekers to follow Him. When Jesus said this, he was referring to the values and ideals that He used His life to embody. He was describing a Path, high and precarious, in sight of the world, protected, but not for the faint of heart. He was not describing *Christianity*, nor inviting people to a tribe where we bond over a shared vocabulary. He was pointing at something universally accessible. Anyone could walk this Path with Him no matter what they identified with, even if it wasn't Christianity. Somehow, paradoxically, walking His Path dissolves the self in such a way that the one identifying with it becomes a walking contradiction. Eventually, it is easier for a camel to pass through the eye of a needle than for a Christian to enter the kingdom of Heaven.

the chasm

Picture two immense lands separated by a deep and treacherous chasm.

For the first many years of life, I did not follow Jesus. I stepped periodically on His Path, but I followed the lead of the world, instead. Eventually, my wandering off the spiritual Path led me to a chasm. I was so fixated on myself that I did not notice the chasm until I was toppling head over heels down into it.

Before I fell, I glimpsed the other side, and I saw the Kingdom. I knew *There* was where I wanted to be. *Here,* the side I had experienced so far, was barren and desolate. There were a few shoddy structures, some hills, some beauty, but it all crumbled upon further inspection like a cheap illusion.

I tumbled down to the bottom of the chasm. When I came to, I was not alone. There were many other lost souls, people who were seeking more but had no idea how to find it.

At rock bottom, we learned of two staircases and a bridge. The staircases were called Grace and Forgiveness, and the bridge was called Religion. The bridge, so the rumors went, would take us into the Kingdom. If it weren't for a sorry sense of belonging in that chasm, many of us would have taken the stairs far sooner than we did. Many refused to believe we deserved our freedom, but after a protracted, self-imposed suffering, I took them step by step. I found my way up and out. But I was still on the wrong side of the chasm. I still needed the Bridge.

Once across the bridge, I stared out at the magnificent land now accessible to me. A Kingdom awaited. It had captured my eyes when I was drunk on myself, when I had taken my great fall, and here I was about to enter. The bridge had delivered me to the Kingdom, safely and soundly. It had suspended me above the pain, suffering, and darkness below, and got me to a place I often doubted was possible for me.

I took my newfound relationship with Christ and set out into the Kingdom with a few others. Before we could take more than a few steps, we were called back. We were told to stay with the bridge, that it was our savior. We were told that one could make a comfortable life living beneath it. We pointed at the vast Kingdom explaining that our destination was elsewhere, but the bridge-dwellers, like trolls, insisted. So, under fire of their shame and misunderstanding, a congregation of us left them behind. We noted as we walked away that the bridge *is* a beautiful construction. It aided in our salvation, but it was always clearly a *bridge*. Its purpose was fulfilled when it brought us across, into a relationship with the Father. Into the Kingdom.

all are welcome

Arrival in the Kingdom does not mean one has gained eternal safety. There is an edge that drops into the chasm on the Kingdom side, too. One can fall into it just as easily, if they are not watching their footing. Thus, it is always imperative that one asks, "*What Path am I on?*"

Each step is either leading you deeper into the Kingdom of relationship or propelling you toward ruin. Shame and misunderstanding might also call you back to living a sheltered, doctrinal existence. The bridge-dwellers may have found their security, but it is not in Christ.

The Christian terminology thus far is intended. I hope for this book to connect with the lovers of Christ who feel like there is so much more out there. Perhaps you are one of them, and you sense that your spiritual relationship is rigid, boring, tiresome, and leaves you feeling the phantom pain of angst that began at our separation from God in the Garden of Eden.

Perhaps this terminology turns you off. This book is also for you. This book is for anyone looking for the way, seeking truth, or craving life. At times I will diverge from the Christian vocabulary with the hope that this will create connections between your highest intuition and scripture in the Bible. It may be that you do not disagree with the Bible after all, but simply, you have developed an affinity for a different way of articulating truth. This is the entire point of this section, to explain that Jesus was not the founder of Christianity. His followers do not put their faith in other Christians, but in Him. While Jesus had his lexicon, and that lexicon has been tarnished, His words ring true when we separate them from the simplistic interpretations that tarnished them in the first place.

Some of us were born with a map to the Kingdom, like the one you will soon be introduced to. We had great parents who held the line and did their best to pass on high values and ideals. Some of us were born in the dark, and had to chop through thickets of thorns to even catch a glimpse of Light. Most importantly, nobody is born in the Kingdom. There are no legacy bids. We all must choose the Path, and then walk it ourselves. The Path to the Kingdom includes the same steps no matter where you start, but understand that nobody is walking with equal ease of access to the Light. Know this, and use this knowledge to appreciate the value of sharing what Light you have.

temporary displacement

Long before I entered the Kingdom, still years before falling into the chasm, I was lost. In the decade leading up to my 2018 chasm-fall, my left foot stepped steadily in **greed** and my right in **worry**. I took shortcuts, thinking they existed. I immersed myself in the world, on the wrong side of the chasm, and became convinced that *this* was all there was. I joined a coterie of like-minded tribesmen and we worked together to fortify ourselves without God. Together we insisted that *our will be done.*

But even though I'd walked to the end of my rope, the one tethering me to the spiritual Path, *and let go*, the rope never let go of me. Despite my best efforts, despite my feelings of inauthenticity, disgust with myself, shame, and condemnation, I was not as lost from the Kingdom as I supposed.

Guidance showed up in the symptoms of my emotional fray. There were certain behaviors that simply could not continue. Greed, worry, and other forces had led me to maligned jobs with misguided leadership. Thankfully, these dark places were not without angels. The guidance of these Lightwielders, each of them grounded in Kingdom-based ideas like love, became my saving grace.

With their help, I decided to quit my job. Quitting my job in 2014, when I had no idea where to go, was a small attempt at refinding the Path.

While I looked for new careers, my wish was for comfort, wealth, security, connection, and recognition. As a 22 year old, I wanted kush. I wanted lavish extravagance, authority, and a nice title. Superficial things. I was still *of the world* very clearly on the material side of the chasm. I was still determined for *my will to be done.* My angels suggested to me that there were better places to plant my feet, but out of habit, out of selfishness, out of fear, out of denial that more existed, my feet still landed in *greed* and *worry*.

An insurance sales recruiter assured me that I would find all of the aforementioned prizes working with his group. So I signed up to sell insurance door-to-door. There were no immediate signs of those things, but they were there, promised, in the distance. While I waited for that day, I got opportunities to find internal comfort, spiritual wealth, security in my abilities, connection to discomfort, and recognition of how God answers prayers. Though I still had a long way to go, this career reminded me of the flavors of the Path. I began to be able to differentiate what is *made* from what is *created*, what is done in *force* versus what is formed from *power*. I began to recognize the importance of noticing what path I tread down. With this awareness, my walk began to change.

This career did not give me what I wanted, but it did give me opportunities to become the man compatible with my desires. Although I entered into it for the wrong reasons, God knew how to use it and I eagerly wanted Him to. Cleverly, He used my strong sense of personal responsibility to create a longing for the Kingdom. I was acutely aware of my shortcomings, which allowed me to admit my humanness, which humbled me, and put me in touch with where He wanted to do His work. Continuously, in countless ways, He pointed me back toward the Path.

From there, one is in the right position to recognize God crafting opportunities to grow. This personal responsibility, now this desire to know God, coaxes me to say *yes* when I want to say *no*, to engage in challenges *because* I am scared, and to never let good enough alone. What I want is not as important to me as what I need. This has led me time and time again to begrudgingly face growth. God will always provide my medicine. I do not always take the medicine happily, but I am not going to deny myself something that I know is for my highest good.

While I wanted kush comfort and substantial wealth, I had not earned it. Various wants are always floating into my awareness. They converge to form this *ideal*, my best idea of the life I dream for myself. I wanted my dreams to be my reality, but I was still a thousand challenges away from being the man who lives those dreams. I could not lie to myself about this fact, nor could I fool the universe that I was ready for it. I still had a lot of developing to do, and this insurance career fit the bill. While I wanted to sit back and revel in a life well lived on the dragon's pile of gold and gemstones, much to my angst, I knew I had yet to face the necessary perils.

I have accepted one of the rules of life: *If you want the pearls of great price, you must face the perils of great strife.*

One thing I know from experience is that *God is into growing His children.* That might be His favorite pastime. He is an active and attentive Father. He knows our potential and He knows our purpose. He wants us to know it, too. To realize it. To fulfill it. He has witnessed the cauldrons of earth and has seen the heat under which precious things are formed. The necessity of the crucible is not lost on Him. He wants us in pursuit of our greatest potential, but He never intended for us to face it alone. He wants us childlike and in complete trust, leaning into who He has made us to be.

Knowing this plants us firmly in the knowledge that life happens *for us.* If this is true then there are no victims in reality who are not victims in their own minds. If you are of the belief that nobody takes care of you better than your Father, then how could anything He orchestrates or allows be wrong? All that has unfolded in our lives can be purposeful. If something seems wrong, it is only wrong in our perception. It is only wrong until we discover why it was necessary. When the lesson is finally learned, when the purpose of our struggle is fulfilled, this truth becomes blissfully obvious.

A detour is merely a diversion from your intended course.

A tourist is a person who is traveling for pleasure.

Throughout this book, you will learn the philosophies of *The Detourist.* A *Detourist* is one who welcomes life with unconditional acceptance, even when reality unfolds starkly different from your preferences. You will learn from your hindsight that your letdowns were just equipping you for future triumphs. As you reflect on your Path, you will come to appreciate your ability to grow, to learn, and to step more wisely. Your failures will take on a new light. Your losses will become lessons. The reasons you have to reject reality will fade away and be replaced by a thirst for transcendence. Your current condition will cease to scare you because you will see that not only are you not *stuck*, but you are already growing the moment you accept yourself. As life twists and turns, no matter where you go, there the Detourist is, in unconditional peace.

Diversions from the Detourist's intended course are met with curiosity, a zest for the unexpected, and complete and utter trust.

a divine trail marker

Six months into my door-to-door insurance job, in February 2015, I was in a car accident. The offender's insurance company refused to accept responsibility. The car sat in the shop for six weeks. Over fifty phone calls to the insurance company yielded no results. In the meantime, I walked business to business in the Chiberian winter. I stuck it out. Finally, I decided to come out of pocket for repairs. The whole experience soured me on Chicago, so as winter lingered into April, I had enough. I needed some breathing room from the tumultuous city, and decided a visit to my friend, Alex, in Florida would do the trick.

"Hey. I want to come visit you," I texted him. "Orlando sounds pretty good about now."

He said, "Yeah, buddy! But I am not in Orlando anymore. I just moved." *Please, nowhere cold.* "I live in Austin, Texas now," he wrote.

"That works."

"Man, you will love Austin," he said. He began to rant and rave about his favorite things. Alex is the type of friend who is always working on a larger sell. "You're probably going to want to move here," he said. He went on, "There are a lot of Michigan State grads here. In fact, I just met this guy the other day. You two would love each other. We were down on Rainey Street being fools, jumping off bars, pulling our shirts over our heads and acting like birds. Funny stuff, man."

"That's amazing," I said, thinking back to my junior and senior years of college. After Alex had transferred from Michigan State to Full Sail in Orlando, he left me in the market for a best friend. The guy that replaced him was named Trent. He was just like Alex but dialed up a few notches. This suited me just fine for my last two years of college. I related my train of thought to Alex, saying, "Sounds like you met my friend Trent."

While waiting for Alex to text back, I thought about Trent. I missed him. Maybe I would visit him, as well. As far as I knew, Trent was in Oklahoma. I had just seen some pictures of him mudding in Tulsa. I messaged him, "Hey, where are you at nowadays?"

Alex messaged back, "Well, the guy's name is Trent."

Trent texted back, "My company just transferred me to Austin!"

Had that car accident been avoided, perhaps I would never have been frustrated enough to text Alex. Maybe my life would have been steered toward Texas by other means. Either way, my move to Austin was not by accident. That synchronicity jolted me into action. It brought me to the place I have called home for eight years. I now see God is more than a strict Father. He was waiting right on the other side of a little grace. He knows me well and He loves me a lot. That love shows up in His ability to speak directly to me, wherever I am looking. He understands my values and my value. He knows what I find interesting, practical, and beautiful. These are the types of things He uses to guide me. Friendship and brotherhood are often His tools. He slows me down with pristine sunsets, He speeds me up with true love, He turns me with dead ends, and He opens me up with interesting people.

Once upon a time a young man pulled his car up to an intersection. He did not know whether he should go left or right. What he did know was that he did not arrive at this intersection by accident. He paused momentarily to look both ways. Each direction was filled with things of varying allure. He looked back and forth, right and left, wrought in contemplation. Then he began to notice a variance in his body when he looked to the left. The road to the right looked safe, but the road to the left brushed him with awe, with beauty, with necessity, with meaning. While there was nothing wrong with right, the leftward way stirred his heart in that familiar way. Without further ado, the young man turned left.

hypothetical dialogue with god

God speaks to me in my internal dialogue, like my highest intuition:

"WHATCHA DOING, MATT?" GOD ASKS.

"KEEPING ON KEEPING ON," I SAY, MY NOSE TO THE GRINDSTONE.

"I SEE THAT. YOU HAVE QUITE A WORK ETHIC. I CAN USE THAT. YOU ARE ALSO SHOWING AMAZING LEVELS OF DEVOTION AND LOYALTY. I WILL DEFINITELY PUT THOSE TO GOOD USE. YOUR STUBBORNNESS IS SECOND TO NONE. IT GIVES YOU THAT DOGGED DETERMINATION TO BELIEVE IN YOURSELF. IT'S CUTE, HONESTLY."

"THANK YOU," I SAY, FEELING CUTE. "I AM NOT ALL THAT HAPPY, THOUGH. MY FRIEND TOLD ME I SHOULD NOT BE SELLING INSURANCE, BUT I SHOULD BE DOING SOMETHING CREATIVE. I CANNOT GET HIS WORDS OUT OF MY HEAD."

GOD NODS. "YOUR FRIEND HAS A POINT."

GOD DOES NOT UNDERSTAND. HE DOES NOW KNOW ABOUT THE VOW. I TELL HIM, "BUT THIS IS THE JOB I SAID I WOULD DO FOREVER. I TOLD SOMEONE THAT ONCE. I SAID IT OUT LOUD. AND SO NOW I AM HELD TO IT."

"YOU JUST SAID THAT TO IMPRESS YOUR BOSS. AND IT GAVE YOU A LITTLE BOOST OF SECURITY," GOD REMINDS ME. "YOU ARE FREE TO MAKE ANY DECISION YOU LIKE."

I BITE MY LIP. "I HAVE A COUPLE DREAMS...BUT THEY SEEM IMPOSSIBLE."

GOD NODS THOUGHTFULLY. "MY SON ONCE SAID, 'WITH MAN THIS IS IMPOSSIBLE, BUT WITH GOD ALL THINGS ARE POSSIBLE.' I HAVE A COUPLE IDEAS FOR YOU, IF MAYBE YOU WANT TO WORK ON THEM TOGETHER?"

I AM SKEPTICAL. "MAYBE..." I TELL HIM STUBBORNLY.

"I THINK YOU WILL LIKE WHAT I HAVE IN MIND," GOD TEASES.

"OKAY. TELL ME ABOUT IT," I REQUEST.

"HOW ABOUT YOU GO OUT AND PLAY IN NATURE? WE WILL TALK ABOUT IT SOON."

God was saying, *remember the Path?* He was inviting me to follow Him to the Kingdom.

If only a conversation like this was all it took. I had spent my entire life *efforting*. I was certain the only way to fulfill my dreams was by forcing them. It was going to take a lot more than an internal conversation with God to buck me from my grind. The idea that there was a loving undercurrent to the world that wanted me to be in love with my life, well, that sounded a bit preposterous. The idea that I could relax, be patient, and allow this undercurrent to carry me in the right direction was not easily believed. I had no idea about *Power*, the sustainable alternative to *Force*. However, the idea did sound enticing...I was running low on energy and quite frankly, I needed to find a more sustainable Source.

God's proposition sat in the back of my mind. While it did, a piece of scripture kept showing up in my life. It appeared through somebody on the phone walking by me on the sidewalk, a poster in a Thai restaurant, my Christian friend talking about what was on his heart. The verse comes from Proverbs.

"Trust in the Lord with all thine heart;
and lean not unto thine own understanding. In all thy ways
acknowledge Him, and He shall direct thy paths."

It seemed to say, "You are *trying* way too hard." Yet my stubbornness prevailed for some time longer. I marched around, still planting feet in greed and worry. Still taking shortcuts. So help me God, I could not get out of my own way!

It was going to take more than blatant synchronicities. It was going to take a massive blessing. God would have to cook up something dramatic, something I could not second guess, some inciting incident I could not easily undo. He sent his goodness down the channel, and when it finally arrived in my reality, it devastated me.

In 2017, because of my poor choices and shortcuts, the insurance company I had worked so hard for let me go. *I got canned!*

Most of us have been fired at some point. In the aftermath I began overthinking everything. I began asking myself what being fired (the fourth time) meant about me. I started telling stories of brokenness. I mourned the specific future with this company that I had become attached to, which was my security. I moped. I cried. I raged. I cursed. At the time, the last thing on my mind was God's craftiness. It took months before I was looking up with playful curiosity asking, "What are you up, *Abba?*"

Also in the aftermath, I seized an opportunity to capture a dream. I moved into a van and traveled the country for a year. I wrote about that experience in my book, *Where the Rubber Meets the Road*. It is the culmination of an era spent adamantly chasing my will. It is the story of me crashing into Jesus. It is a story of love, adventure, heartache, and salvation. In that story, where the rubber met the road, He showed me that He can use everything. Nothing is ever wasted. He brought me out like a champion, arms raised, grateful.

"And we know that in all things God works for the good of those who love him, who have been called according to his purpose."

By the time I could appreciate the beauty of His thrifty work, I was 29 and it was 2019. I had lived enough life to begin to recognize a pattern. Looking back at my past devastations, one thing was apparent. Everything always works out. My aunt had supplied our family with fridge magnets with a simple message: "Everything works out in the end. If it hasn't worked out, it isn't the end." With this simple truth in mind, can we let our hindsight become foresight? Can we keep our hearts open as we weather these apparent devastations? Can we know that this too shall pass? Great things and struggles pass. Eventually, they are resolved. Can this little bit of knowledge grant us peace when our life situation seems bleak? Can we accept how little we will ever know about what God is up to and just enjoy the ride, detours and all?

Everything always works out.

introduction

Everything always works out.

That is the mantra of The Detourist. As life twists and turns, *taking detours*, the Detourist can see that this is God's most direct route. It is our humanness, our egos, that insist we can see the entire picture when we are merely focused on a small smudge. God sees the big picture. God sees the danger up ahead, the beauty of the backroads, the fun you will have kicking up country dust. He knows where He has hidden all the Another Man's Treasure.

To live in love with life in this way requires trust. It requires surrender. You get to relinquish control. You get to fall into alignment with Power.

Through this book, we are going to explore the truth.

We are going to zoom out and take a look at the world through the eyes of God. We are going to gaze upon the entire kaleidoscope of reality. We are going to retreat from our ideas of ourselves and our existence. We are going to explore concepts on the brink of science and spirituality. We will wind our way through topics from quantum physics, the law of attraction, consciousness, belief, creation energy, and willpower. We will talk about Jesus Christ. We will get to see how all of these things are connected. We are going to become aware of the power of our thoughts. With the best of intentions, we will realize what it means to be created in the image of God.

If we consult the map, we see we are starting *Here*. We always must start exactly where we are: *Here*, now. We will end *There*. Here and There appear right next to each other on the map. Physically, they might be in the same place. However, I assure you they could not be more different.

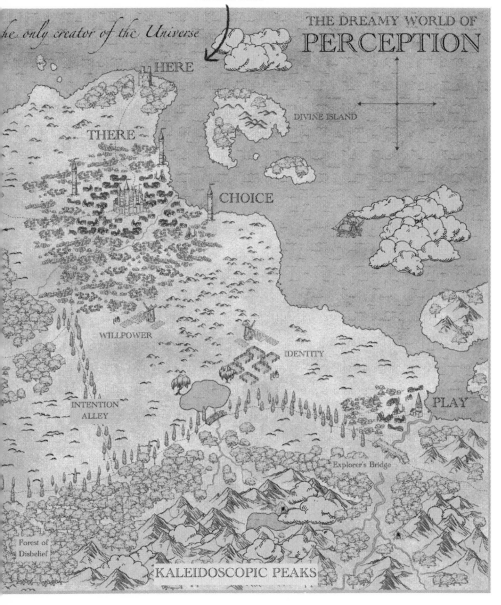

One cannot get There from Here without a personal journey. It can be perilous at times, but nobody who ever arrived There regrets it. It is the nearest thing to heaven on Earth. *There* is a utopia. You will know you have arrived There because it is fresh and bright. From the perspective of Here, There seems a mystical, magical, make-believe place. It is. It is also indubitably real.

"Heaven and Hell are only a tenth of an inch apart."

— ZEN

Before we set out, there is one thing we must remember along the way. It is essential to our survival and our arrival. In the world of *The Detourist*, everything we believe *will and does* become manifest. If we believe in monsters, we will encounter monsters. If we believe in abundance, we will bask in riches. If we believe in salvation, we will encounter a Savior. Some call this the law of attraction. It is, in part. Along the way, this idea will become our constant partner.

The fine print on the bottom of our trail map reads: *God is not the only creator of the universe*. We, human beings, also possess the ability to project our thoughts into the material universe. We are after all, created in *the Creator's* image. We all come together with the Lord as co-creators of reality. Like God's, your beliefs become manifest in the material world. It may have escaped your notice thus far. There *is* a slight lag between belief and materialization. Reflect and you will see that it is true. Reflect and see that your beliefs in fear, hope, love, beauty, splendor, health, sickness, etc., when they were not contradictory, have always proven out.

"So God created man in His own image."

God gave man imagination for a reason. Erwin McManus sees imagination as our God-image. He says that humans deal in futures. Right now you are living inside God's and another's imagination. God first imagined the nature outside, and a person first imagined the decor of every room you have ever been in. Decor is so much more than materials.

Mary Daly said, "It is the Creative potential itself that is the image of God."

This is both a scary and encouraging prospect. As co-creators within a loving God, we have a lot of power in our thoughts and our beliefs, which comes with a need for ownership and personal responsibility. No person ever attained self mastery with cheap spiritual mind tricks. As frightening as taking complete ownership of our part in the co-creation can be, it is preferable to viewing ourselves as victims of happenstance. Ownership is like a battery. It is not always included, but you need it for this all to work.

Here is a story about ownership.

In October 2019, my grandmother passed away.

My extended family members are now all scattered across the globe. We seldom get together anymore. The funeral was somber, naturally, but everyone was too busy hugging each other to be too sad. Our funniest stories were exchanged. Recounting stories of childhood in a place of childhood brought out the youth in us all. We imagined grandma in her heaven, riding a Schwinn beach-cruiser bicycle through an eternal, endlessly variant wildlife refuge.

Back at grandpa's house, the youngest were pulled behind the tractor in a soapbox car. The cousins got a workout in with grandpa's ancient, rusty weight set. Everyone joined in on a massive ultimate frisbee match. One of my larger cousins laid me out, but hurt himself. We finished the day gathered around a big table strewn with nostalgic foods.

But the good times pass just as truly as the hard times. Eventually it was time to say goodbyes. Grandpa was going to be staying at my parents' house indefinitely, so dad, grandpa, and I hopped in a car together.

It was not until we were driving away from grandpa's house that reality began settling in. It seemed that was happening for everyone. For the first ten minutes of the car ride, we sat in thoughtful silence.

Until we passed through my dad's hometown. He grew up in the middle of Michigan in a farming town called Sheridan. The highway we drove on was two lanes, one in each direction. Traffic on this highway raced in both directions down the long, straight, flat road through corn fields.

A couple miles outside of town, we noticed something in the road up ahead. As we got closer, we saw it was twenty somethings. They were pink blobs that as we approached grew faces and little teddy-bear bodies. My dad threw on his hazards and began to pull over.

"What are you doing, dad?" I asked.

He took a second to respond. "Picking up this stuff." He pulled the car into the ditch and got out. Cars continued to fly by in either direction.

I got out of the car to question him. "Why?"

"Somebody must have lost a bunch of stuffed animals," he said, picking one up.

That did not answer my question.

"Dad, are you sure this is a good idea?" I questioned. He dashed out into the street and picked up a few before any cars could get close. After being at the funeral earlier that day, death seemed a little too close. I would have rather not taken a risk just to pick up some lost toys. "There are a lot of cars," I said.

He heard me, but stayed focused on the task at hand.

"I grew up on this road, Matt," he said.

At the time what I heard was his attempt at pacifying me. Reassuring me. It worked. I suddenly saw him a little differently. As though his childhood was spent playing frogger on this very highway. It seemed he was telling me to trust him.

The more I thought about it, however, the more something else became apparent. We drove the rest of the way home and we did not stop anywhere else to pick up any trash. In fact, in the tens of thousands of driven miles for which I was his passenger, he had never picked up anything on the side of the street before. *So why here and why now?*

I grew up on this road, Matt, he had said. There was something different about this road than all the others. He grew up on that road. It had been forty years since he had lived on that road, but time had not diminished the ownership he felt toward it.

This is his road, and while he draws breath, he will remain its steward.

Ownership presents us with a very special opportunity. When we own something, we tend to take particular care of it. It is nobody else's responsibility but ours. This is why Jesus stood at the well with the Samaritan woman saying, "If you knew the gift of God and who it is that asks you for a drink, you would have asked Him and he would have given you *living water*." The Samaritan woman, and every other person, must take ownership of their own well-being. Of their own salvation. Nobody can accept these things on our behalf, no matter how much the Gifter wishes to give them to us.

If you bought this book for yourself, props to you. As the owner of this book, you are also the proud owner of the opportunity to adopt the lessons within. If you would pardon me for being crass, people who read books without any intentional implementation are merely mentally or spiritually masturbating. Nothing is made. Nothing is gained. A whole lot of potential creation energy gets squandered. I wrote this book with the desire for you to experience a magnification. The one who is magnified most by this journey is the one who experiments with these ideas, trying them on for one's self. This is intended to be an exploration of your relationship to the divine within and without. If done with intention, the ideas in this book will ripen many fruits for you. *If done with intention*. If approached with ownership.

choice

Another gift of our creator is choice. Free will. Genesis 4:7 says, "[sin] desires to have you, but *you may* rule over it." *Timshel*.

At the very core of all decisions is our *choice* to follow our deep divinity or our shallow individuality. We may *choose* our own path. We are the owners of our destiny. William Ernest Henley, in his poem *Invictus* states, "I am the master of my fate, I am the captain of my soul."

Choice is yours.

Along the journey of *The Detourist*, it is your responsibility to mind your side of the street. Take ownership of yourself, of your thoughts, of your beliefs, of your health, and of all the rest. If you catch yourself more concerned with the condition of someone else's street, be aware that immediately the litter has begun piling up on your own. Nobody has the ability to focus on another and still give their own evolution its due diligence.

The Detourist offers a journey of self mastery. I will be on this journey long after this book is published. The journey is eternal, as we all are eternally unfinished works of art. Sometimes I have been tempted to believe I have *arrived*, only to have my life circumstances shift and more work is revealed. It is healthy to ask, especially in good times: *How deep is my sainthood, really?*

To be human means we are enraptured in a dance between our duality and our divinity. Sometimes we co-create with a loving God, and sometimes we make with our shallow egos. The journey of self mastery is one of observation instead of evaluation. It is one of discernment. Along the way we must do our best to recognize when we are in alignment with Peace or our shallowness. From *Here* we use our abilities to see, to accept, to cope, to resolve, to learn, to grow, to change, and to evolve. This is not often a comfortable process. By seeking this discomfort, we change its meaning in our lives. By seeking evolution, we recognize that we are not stuck. By being and thinking differently, we can invite more of what we want and less of what we do not. On the journey to *There*, the most important step is the next one.

This is a burden I bear enthusiastically. I would have it no other way.

an exercise in gratitude

I have had a conflicting relationship with photography. Is living in the moment the right answer? Or is preserving the moment on film more everlasting?

If you have ever been to a festival or a concert, you have seen people filming the performance on their phones. You may have been one of those people, at some point. Or you may have commented about how silly that seems, missing the show to film it. *Do these people go home and watch their twenty minute Red Hot Chili Peppers video?* I certainly never have.

But I have also taken two thousand mile road trips and neglected to take a single picture. Then months after the trip, my memory is all I have. I comb through my memories with some effort, but the colors of the California coastline escape me, the tree branches in Olympic National Park heavy under rain cannot be called crispy back to recollection, the detail of stretching Arizona deserts speckled pink with prickly pear have faded to gray...

Do I wish to live so deeply in the present that I never waste time with nostalgia? Or do I wish to live a rich life of adventure that, in its more mundane moments, I have photographic totems to call up memories of grandeur?

And then I had a revelation about the practice of photography. Taking pictures is an exercise in appreciation. When you point your camera, your subject is set aside. The act of pointing your camera at something identifies it, holds it, appreciates it. It is one thing to notice worthiness, but another thing altogether to stop and give the worthiness your attention. The more you pause when you notice beauty, the more you slow to notice more. The tendency strengthens like a muscle. You will find yourself appreciating nuances that you had previously missed, on account of looking more deeply. When you slow down to look more deeply, you feel more deeply. Life and the beauty within it become etched in metal memory. And you have a totem to call the distinct memory forward.

When you pause to take a picture, you are not stepping back and away. You are not retreating out of the present. You are immersing yourself into the scene. You are tying a chord of gratitude between you and it, and in doing thus, becoming one with it. You recognize the beauty not as something separate from yourself, but as part of yourself. Beauty is within the beholder. If you spot it, you got it. The more you see beauty, the more beautiful you are.

Let's take a moment to practice.

Go find your phone or your camera. You are going to take seven pictures. You will take one for each color of the rainbow, plus black.

Go around your setting with your camera and take a picture with a red, orange, yellow, green, blue, violet and black subject. *Become Roy G. Biv, famous photographer.* Take your time seeking out the perfect subject. Maybe you find a blue ring from a milk carton cast against the stark black asphalt. They do not have to be beautiful objects, merely objects you find beauty in. Notice them, and know that when you do, you are inviting a sense of beauty and wonder inside yourself. The slowing down, the intention we have set, and the attention you offer is all the recipe for immersive gratitude.

Go!

If you wish to spice things up, find a partner! Make it fun! Make it a competition where family and friends vote on whose picture is better. But remember, *better* is highly subjective. Beauty is, after all, within the beholder. If someone tells you your pictures are crap, pray for them.

❖ ❖ ❖

Many of the concepts with The Detourist can
be integrated with exercises like this.

If you are interested in a
14 Day Awareness Expanding Game,

go to **www.matthewemmorey.com/Collideoscope**
to download the free companion.

part one

trust

song of
the universal

by Walt Whitman

1.

COME SAID THE MUSE,
SING ME A SONG NO POET YET HAS CHANTED,
SING ME THE UNIVERSAL.

IN THIS BROAD EARTH OF OURS,
AMID THE MEASURELESS GROSSNESS AND THE SLAG,
ENCLOSED AND SAFE WITHIN ITS CENTRAL HEART,
NESTLES THE SEED PERFECTION.

BY EVERY LIFE A SHARE OR MORE OR LESS,
NONE BORN BUT IT IS BORN, CONCEAL'D OR UNCONCEAL'D
THE SEED IS WAITING.

2.

LO! KEEN-EYED TOWERING SCIENCE,
AS FROM TALL PEAKS THE MODERN OVERLOOKING,
SUCCESSIVE ABSOLUTE FIATS ISSUING.

YET AGAIN, LO! THE SOUL, ABOVE ALL SCIENCE,
FOR IT HAS HISTORY GATHER'D LIKE HUSKS AROUND THE GLOBE,
FOR IT THE ENTIRE STAR-MYRIADS ROLL THROUGH THE SKY.

IN SPIRAL ROUTES BY LONG DETOURS,
(AS A MUCH-TACKING SHIP UPON THE SEA,)
FOR IT THE PARTIAL TO THE PERMANENT FLOWING,
FOR IT THE REAL TO THE IDEAL TENDS.

FOR IT THE MYSTIC EVOLUTION,
NOT THE RIGHT ONLY JUSTIFIED, WHAT WE CALL EVIL ALSO JUSTIFIED.

FORTH FROM THEIR MASKS, NO MATTER WHAT,
FROM THE HUGE FESTERING TRUNK, FROM CRAFT AND GUILE AND TEARS,
HEALTH TO EMERGE AND JOY, JOY UNIVERSAL.

OUT OF THE BULK, THE MORBID AND THE SHALLOW,
OUT OF THE BAD MAJORITY, THE VARIED COUNTLESS FRAUDS OF MEN AND
STATES,
ELECTRIC, ANTISEPTIC YET, CLEAVING, SUFFUSING ALL,
ONLY THE GOOD IS UNIVERSAL.

CHAPTER 1

belief

---

the case for an intelligent, intentional and loving creator

I used to divide people into two belief systems: "Seeing is Believing" and "Believing is Seeing". The Detourist knows that both are true, once you know where to look.

Seeing is Believing people walk by sight.

For example, a friend of mine stayed with me the weekend after I had been traveling with my girlfriend for a week. The two of us hung out all weekend without disruption. At the end of that weekend, my friend said, "It doesn't seem like you really see your girlfriend that much…" I laughed. I told him again of the entire week we just spent traveling together. This friend happens to be a staunch atheist. When we disagree I often have to remind him of something that he did not see. He knew about our travels together, but for him, seeing is believing.

Believing is Seeing people walk by faith.

There is an obvious distinction. Anyone who learns a new word and then hears it soon after, or learns of a new concept and then witnesses it in the wild knows that sometimes, becoming aware of the existence of something allows it to appear. This is why behavioral psychologists say "If you spot it, you got it." While the statement is simplistic in the way it defines having it, being aware of a thing *is* a prerequisite for seeing it - even if those two events are essentially synchronous.

There is a shortcut between the two camps. That shortcut is called *knowing where to look*. If you know where to look, then you can witness the mystical for yourself. Having seen something that defies belief, one is best to embrace the necessary alterations in their belief system.

the electromagnetic bubble of likeness

Let us look at some of the mystical properties of water.

I bought a house in June 2021. When I first moved in, for the first five days, I did not have water. The refuse I created was a little greater that week - napkins, paper plates, plastic cups, disposable tableware - and still, dishes piled up in the sink.

Without water, I could not make anything clean. Not myself, not the dishes, not the floors. In its absence, I thought about the importance of water. I considered how unnerving a vast, empty desert is for humankind. I thought about how reassured I feel next to rivers and lakes. I thought about its presence throughout the entirety of human evolution, and about how my body is as much as 75% water.

When the water finally came on, I cleaned up. It occurred to me that water is so vital that its presence is simultaneously nothingness. *Clean* means covered in water. Water is so neutral that its existence can be overlooked. Its absence, however, can never be.

As neutral as it is, not all water is created equal. In fact, water is very impressionable. Under the wrong impression, water can become flat and lifeless.

Under the right impression, water is life. When you separate its molecules, you get rocket fuel and something highly flammable. Together, though, in the right balance, we cannot live without it.

How we treat our water is how we treat ourselves. The world around us is very impressionable. We are not alone in experiencing our actions, nor are we alone in experiencing our thoughts.

Jesus would have known this when he delivered the Sermon on the Mount. He said, "You have heard that it was said to the people long ago, 'You shall not murder, and anyone who murders will be subject to judgment.' But I tell you that anyone who is angry with a brother or sister will be subject to judgment." A few verses later, he says, "You have heard that it was said, 'You shall not commit adultery.' But I tell you that anyone who looks at another lustfully has already committed adultery with them in their heart." This was as radical a message in Jesus' time as it is today. It might have been even more radical then, without quantum physics to elucidate his meaning. Or without the research of people like Dr. Masaru Emoto.

The work of Dr. Masaru Emoto in his book, *The Hidden Messages of Water*, had shown that molecules of water subjected to loving intention freeze in the form of brilliant, complex, and colorful crystals.

Dr. Masaru conducted his experiment by filling jars with water. He labeled them the corresponding message and then by meditating in the presence of these jars with these deliberate intentions, the doctor exposed them to the respective energies. Almost immediately, he observed the following changes.

THANK YOU | WISDOM | TRUTH | ETERNAL
ANGEL | I LOVE YOU | PEACE | YOU FOOL
YOU MAKE ME SICK | EVIL | POLLUTED WATER BEFORE PRAYER | POLLUTED WATER AFTER PRAYER

He later decided to take his experiment a bit more seriously, ensuring that his experiments were less vulnerable to scientific scrutiny. He put large amounts of water in jars and added rice, in what would become his famous Rice Experiment. He created three identical jars, labeled two of them with the phrases "Thank you" and "You are an idiot". He left the third one blank. Everyday for 30 days he visited each jar for a minute where he read the corresponding message. Day by day, he tracked the changes in the jars. By the end of the month, he noticed the water in the jar labeled "Thank you" had started to ferment and was giving off a pleasant odor. "You are an idiot" turned black and took on a rotted shape. The jar left blank that had been ignored the entire time turned a nasty green-blue color.

Of course, the words these droplets of water are exposed to are less important than the energy behind the words. Humans are vibrational beings, and water is vibrationally impressionable.

Dr. Emoto's work proves two things. The first, is that different intentions carry different vibrational signatures. This pertains to Jesus's sermon because one does not need to act on their aggression for the molecules around them to be affected by it. The second thing it proves is that we are not alone in experiencing our thoughts. To feel anger, lust, love, or compassion is to surround ourselves in an electromagnetic bubble of likeness.

atomic intention

This is the power of intention on the molecular level. Let's take a look at the same thing on the atomic level.

My elementary school teachers all lied to me.

Especially the science teachers.

They did not mean to. They taught out of textbooks that were doing their best with what we "knew" at the time. This was twenty years ago, in the 90s, but this inaccuracy is still being taught in schools today. Despite quantum leaps in scientific understanding, a lasting reverence to Newton's Laws undermines many of these modern revelations.

I don't remember any science teacher opening class with the caveat, "Now, listen class. I want you to learn all of this, all of it will be on the test, but don't cling too tightly to it. We are starting to suspect that all of this...*might be wrong*. Oh, and these tests with which you are tested on all this potentially wrong knowledge will be used to determine your intelligence! We are going to give you scores to identify with! So remember this stuff! But definitely be prepared to forget it."

Science deals in theories. Science itself is a process. Science is decided by people called scientists, and like all people, they are not without their stubborn and outmoded beliefs. Suffice it to say that while we have a lot of confidence, in the grand scheme, we know very little.

One instance of learning a theory that has been modified since, is the electron.

In school we were taught about the material universe. It was all quite Newtonian. The physical world we live in is also called *spacetime reality*. The matter in spacetime reality includes everything that you know: that lamp, this book, your bookmark, *yourself*. If there are atoms involved, it is a substance of the material universe. It has mass. It is matter. It is measurable. Isaac Newton identified some laws that governed these substances.

We were taught that an electron is matter, and thereby a constant part of spacetime reality. We were taught that it orbits the nucleus of an atom, in an orbital. Atoms, the building blocks of larger matter, have three parts. Protons, neutrons, and electrons. Protons and neutrons make up the nucleus. These two parts form one material center. Their negatively charged counterpart, the electron, was said to be whirring around the outside, balancing out the charge of the atom.

Here is where I was miseducated. An electron is different. Sometimes it is matter, but sometimes it is pure energy. Instead of being a particle, it is merely a negative charge. It is not *always* matter, as I was taught. Sometimes, it is just *pure energy*.

When an electron is energy, it belongs to a sea of similar nothingness that exists everywhere, called the quantum field.

The quantum field is the counterpart to the material universe. It is a background of energy. Max Planck, the father of quantum theory, also called this field *the Matrix*. Because this field is not physical, meaning it contains no matter, it does not conform to physical laws. In the material universe, *stuff* is governed by laws. Sir Isaac Newton identified a list of laws that apply to matter. One such law states that matter cannot travel faster than the speed of light. Pure energy is not bound by the same restrictions. In the quantum field, energy can communicate instantaneously. When communication happens instantly at two points in the field, it stands to reason that what appears to be separate is actually one, unified field. This is another name for the quantum, the Unified Field. It is not a *thing*. It is a field of energy. It is *no thing*, but it is not nothing. It is *Potentiality*.

Electrons do not exist as orbiting particles, as we once thought. They are not a constant member of the material universe. They tend to exist as waves of negatively charged energy in this unified field. A wave is not a thing. A wave is pure energy. A particle is a thing. Therefore, the energy that comprises an electron is usually free. Something needs to happen in order to collapse that energy out of a wave, and into a particle. Something needs to happen to take this background of potential and to define it.

Amazingly, one of those *things* that collapses electron-energy into particles is *mental intention*. Belief.

This fact was happened upon by a group of unsuspecting scientists. They noticed that everywhere they looked for the electron, they found it. They could deduce from the atomic information of the nucleus that there could not possibly be electrons in all places, as protons and electrons existed in balance with each other in regular elements. But the fact remains, everywhere they looked for an electron, there one was. The act of looking, with the intention of finding, made it so. Their mental intention was powerful enough to convert pure energy into matter.

Just like the experiment with Dr. Emoto, theirs show that intentions affect the stuff around us. What is true on a molecular level is also true on an atomic level.

Now let's imagine this microscopic phenomenon on a macrocosmic scale. The Big Bang Theory is how astronomers explain the way the universe began. Since the beginning of time, our universe has been expanding and cooling. In that time, all matter would have been exposed to the four fundamental forces.

1. Gravity
2. Electromagnetism
3. Weak-nuclear force
4. Strong nuclear force

It is supposed that at some point, the Earth became a primordial soup ripe for the initiation of life. The temperature and conditions were ideal, and life spontaneously sprang forth. For some, this may be a reasonable enough explanation. But in order to dissect this, it's important to understand the nature of Earth's earliest life forms.

They were microbes, also known as *dawn bacteria*: microscopic single-celled organisms that did not have a distinct nucleus with a membrane nor other specialized organelles. They were prokaryotes. 1.5 billion years later, eukaryotes showed up. Eukaryotes are organisms whose cells contain a nucleus and other membrane-bound organelles. There is a wide range of eukaryotic organisms, including all animals, plants, fungi, and protists, as well as most algae. Eukaryotes may be either single-celled or multicellular. In order for multicellular organisms to come about, you must have cooperative cells who join together for the betterment of the whole, who designate cellular specialties, and begin constructing a means of passing on their genetic learning.

In the span of 1.5 billion years, Earth goes from being host to something mundane (a soup of hot rocks) to something alive, intentional, cooperative, and intelligent.

How do we go from matter haphazardly exposed to the four fundamental forces to single-celled organisms with intelligence and genetic material? Is the theory of spontaneous arrival enough for you? Personally, I am left with three important, unanswered questions.

My first question is, *"Why this life?"*

My next question is *"Where did the intelligence come from?"*

Then, as we study the behavior of single-celled organisms, we find a desire to survive. We find a spirit of collaboration. We find that at life's most basic level, cooperation is king. These cells came together to cooperate to ensure the survival of the whole. If the nature of nature was not cooperative, we would never have progressed to multicellular organisms, nor eventually to the 30-trillion celled organisms that humans are today.

My last question is, *"What well of power were they drawing from?"*

On that scale, this is evidence of a conscious Creator. It is evidence that underlying everything we see, there is an existence of an intentional and intelligent mind. In an entropic system, some things are advancing further into chaos while others are becoming highly organized, cooperative, and advanced. Be that intention alone influences the world electromagnetically, all we need to answer those three questions is a Mind capable of intending.

Hebrews 11:3 reads, *"By faith we understand that the universe was created by the word of God, so that what is seen was not made out of things that are visible."* The *seen* is formed out of the *unseen*.

Why this life? Intention is what collapses potential energy into the specific forms we see around us today.

Where did the intelligence come from? The more we study cells, the more we marvel at their complexity. The four fundamental forces are merely forces. Alone, they do not account for intelligent organization.

What well of power were they drawing from? We can understand a lot about our Creator by taking a look at life in its basic form. We see that life is imbued with a sense of love, community, and unification.

THE MOST DETAILED PHOTOGRAPH OF A CELL TO DATE (2022)

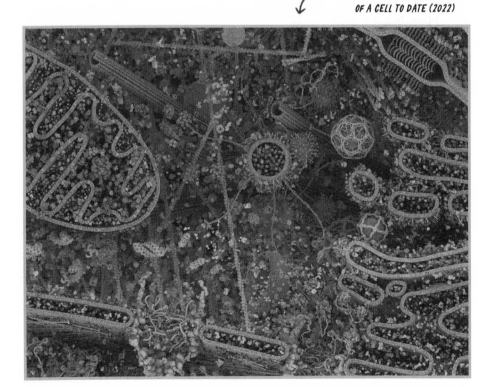

The creation story in the Bible is one way of trying to articulate truth. I do not intend to use this book to try to prove the Bible. Instead, I point at our mystical reality. From here, we do not have to blindly accept the biblical explanations. Instead, we reconcile reality with scientific revelations with biblical explanation. As long as we remain detached from simplistic interpretations of the Bible, we find that all of these are in agreement.

"In the beginning was the Word, and the Word was with God, and the Word was God."

We are vibrational beings.

Words themselves are merely vibrations interpreted by our eardrums.

All stuff also has its vibrational signature, only it vibrates below the range of human audibility. One way to interpret this verse is to say that all Creation was held within God, latent, as potential, awaiting the day He would speak. Of course, He doesn't have to speak per se. *He only has to intend.*

In the material universe, there is infinite space. We have all kicked back and looked up at the stars at some point. It is easy to begin to marvel at the endlessness of the universe. It goes on and on seemingly forever. With some complex, but understandable mathematics, we can determine that our universe is nearly 14 billion years old. At the edge of the distance light has traveled in that time, we are unable to know what lies beyond. As far as we are aware, it is an endless, infinite space.

In quantum reality, there is infinite time. That is because from any present moment, every possible reality exists simultaneously. That is the nature of the quantum field, ready at a moment's intention to collapse energy into reality. The potential is there in the background, waiting, simultaneously existing, stacked on top of one another ad infinitum. Endless, infinite time.

The power that shapes our world is held by a consciousness larger than comprehension, one powerful enough for its intentions to shape the universe as we know it.

Reread Genesis with a curiosity on *how* God created the Heavens and the Earth. As is true in the reality we know, first one must have an idea before anything can become manifest. The tools of God, the power behind His creation, are not hands. We were created in *God's* image, He was not created in ours. God uses His mind to create, to collapse energy into reality. God has an idea, and it springs to life. Later, Jesus takes water and intends it to be wine. God is an omniscient consciousness. God is a mind that can shape the fabric of the cosmos through mere intentions. As He does in Genesis.

> FOR A FULL TEXT OF THE CREATION STORY TOLD IN GENESIS 1-31, JUMP AHEAD TO THE RESOURCES (ON PAGE 247). AS YOU READ, TRY NOT TO ANTHROPOMORPHIZE (PERSONIFY) GOD. TRY NOT TO THINK OF GOD AS THE FIGURE YOU HEAR ABOUT IN RELIGIOUS CONTEXTS. INSTEAD, IMAGINE GOD AS THE ORGANIZING POWER BEHIND CREATION.

In every instance of God's creation, He first has the idea. God creates with His loving, creationist's mind. He imbues His creation with free will, and an essence of Himself. In the case of man, He created in His own image.

What is meant by this line, is that man too has the ability to project his thoughts in the material universe. We saw this truth in Dr. Emoto's work, as well as within the accidental discovery by the scientists, regarding electrons. In other words, man's intentions will collapse energy from waves into particles. Man's mind will be able to pull reality out of potential energy in accord with the intentions held by his God-image. These creations, just as God's creations, maintain a freeness of will. We are made in God's image, with godlike imagination.

Everything that exists first existed in either God's or man's imagination. The nature that is so beautifully constructed came from God's. The cover of this book was first imagined by my cover designer. The clothes you wear, the car you drive, the streets you drive down, the signs you follow...all of these things first existed in someone's imagination before they existed in reality. This is life in God's image.

As a side thought, as Genesis 1:26-30 lays out, we have the privilege of procreation, the role of subduing and ruling, and a status in the garden serving sacred space. The creation account gives humans their identity but also specifies our connectivity to everything around us. Sometimes I wonder if we are like the humans of old, prone to egotistical notions of self-importance. We once believed that the universe revolves around Earth. We fought back Copernicus' idea that the Earth revolved around the sun. We are told, "...have dominion over the fish of the sea, and over the fowl of the air, and over every living thing that moveth upon the earth." Having dominion surely does not mean devalue and mistreat. Knowing that this arrangement was formed by the mind of God, a mind that knows all his creations, such as it is in the case of His sparrows, "...not one of them is forgotten in God's sight," this supposes that we are stewards of God's creatures, more than overlords. I am not a vegetarian myself, but I find it curious that in Genesis 28, our dominion is noted over animals, which is quite different from 29-30, where fruits, seeds, and vegetation is specifically called *meat*. Perhaps my love for grilling is blocking a valuable revelation...For now, I can only reconcile my love for eating animals with a desire to pay the necessary psychic price...by being the one to raise and butcher them. More on this later.

Jesus broke bread with men and said, "This is my body that is for you," and bread changed. It became Love. Whether it is the consecrated host for consumption or the energy of the unified field, our Creator has given us dominion. This is the power that we all have. It is the power to change the fabric of the world with our thoughts. Our power is not in the potency that our savior had, but it is ours nonetheless. What if all of mankind merged good intentions together? While it would still be finite and insignificant in comparison to God, imagine what could be instantaneously solved?

Are you imagining? You are using the power of Belief.

Think of it in these terms.

Imagine that every human on Earth stopped believing in McDonalds. Or even a strong majority. Their disbelief is so absolute that when they drive by the famous golden arches, nothing registers. There may as well be an empty field. Employees would begin looking for new work. Travelers would drive past all their locations. Their burgers would harden and stale. Well, maybe not. But the longevity of their offerings aside, one would satiate his or her beef hankering elsewhere. The lights would soon be off. McDonalds would cease to exist on planet Earth in a matter of months.

The materialization lags shortly behind belief. What we see in reality is our past beliefs reinforced. Material reality is merely the thin skin of potentiality.

The delay is much less with a mind like Jesus. Jesus has the authority to turn water into wine without challenge. As one eternally with God, would He not have the same power as God? Were they not One in the same? These miracles have no degree of magnitude, to our Savior and Creator. A miracle is just a thought like any other. What can be conceived in the mind can be achieved, it is said. In fact, conception is prerequisite. The expression might be reworded, *"What is conceived in the mind and then believed in, is created."*

Of course, it is healthy to maintain an accurate view of mankind versus Christ. We may be redeemed, but we are finite. The ideas we have that promote the good, true, and beautiful are grounded ultimately in the true source of what is good, true, and beautiful. We are not the source, as He is.

In the ideas that follow, it is necessary to recognize our access to power while understanding the fact above. We are actively shaping the world around us, but we must cling tightly to humility.

Put something in your mind and believe in it with *love* and the charge of *desire*. Allow this loving intention to overflow into all facets of your life, until *You* disappears. Get carried away into acts of service. Before long, observe that this belief has become manifest.

Going forward, you enter into life in a dance of co-creation. As I stated in the Introduction, trying to enforce your own will on the world does little good if you are out of alignment with God's loving consciousness. God is the only Creator. When I say we are co-creating, we are like fish splashing a bit of river water onto shore. We do not control the river, its flow, its direction, or its speed. Just because we played a role in splashing the water does not mean that we created those plants that grew because of our efforts. Yet to the plants, to the wildlife that consume the plants, and all the other benefits that ensue, *we do make a difference.*

creating vs. making

Allow me to differentiate between making and creating. God creates. Man can play a role in *creation* when he or she is aligned with the spirit of God, but man is finite. More often, man *makes*.

Creating is the formation of something new. It uses power. It is eternal.

Making is the manipulation of existing materials. It used force. It is highly impermanent.

As we know, man has knowledge of good and evil. Man has the ability to co-create with the source of all that is good, true, and beautiful. Man also has the ability to make with evil thoughts. Any evil thought is inherently out of alignment with our loving Creator. You could reconsider evil to be the absence of our Creator. Making in the absence of God is in your ability as a free-willed, sovereign human being. However, there is no rest for the wicked, meaning any illusion that goes against the Good of God must be meticulously maintained. Evil is only ever made, never created. It has a short shelf life.

Keep believing in love. Love is the essence of the Creator Himself. What you create in love is formed with creation energy, and is created in reality. *It is eternal in its effects.* What is made without love is like a sandcastle on the shore. His loving tide will quickly reduce it to nothingness, fading it to memory, leaving you to wonder if it ever really existed.

As this idea sinks in, you will begin to see a net positivity to all the manifestations around you. There is love in everything that goes around. Though evil beliefs can and do make devastation in our lives, the nature of nature prevents evil from winning out. God is inevitable. Our minds will eventually return to a oneness with His, and we will see that there was a love greater than the evil tucked within. Think, even war gives mankind the opportunity to express courage, to leave their individuality behind, and to die to themselves. If the most heinous nightmares are purposeful for human evolution, what isn't?

In summary: There is a power to the universe. It is the power that collects matter out of potential energy and organizes it into life. That power is the reason why some aspects of the universe progress into chaos and others coalesce upward into higher consciousness. That power is intentional. That power is intelligent. That power is eager for you to know it. That power is Love.

I call Him God.

the nature of nature

What is the nature of nature?
Is it self-serving? Is it mighty?
Is it every man for themself
Bound in thick musculature?
At the very core of existence
Is there a competition?
Is it survival of the fittest
To go the genetic distance?
On what terms are we engaged
In life's infinite game?
Do we stand on a playground?
A battlefield? Or is it a stage?
What is the nature of nature?
Is it indifferent? Is it mindless?

Are these manifestations of random
Until they meet their erasure?
Is life mere borrowed fertilizer
Busy arising and dying
Going on without purpose
Ignorant and none the wiser?
Of this I see no evidence
But in the minds of pessimists
Who see the form and nothing more
Sums equal to their elements...
What is the nature of nature?
With what intention is life created?
What is the attitude of God?
What is the disposition of the maker?
Is all life Gods deliberate design
Each with a fate and a pair of its kind?
A path laid out from birth to grave
Straight - only appearing to wind?
Is nature organized and neat
With rule and order all complete
With an underpin of natural law
Where what ye measure ye always mete?
What is the nature of nature?
Above and beyond what's written on paper
What can we learn from living?
What from the Word come from the manger?
With what string is tied the eternal knot
What vibration when it's plucked?
When consciousness has an idea

What is imbued within Its thoughts
Is life a burst of spontaneity
A mix of light and curiosity
Free will with individuality
Sewn with the divinity of the deity
Subtract the invention of separation
From the essential calculation
And find the difference of relations
Between creator and all incarnations
What is the nature of nature?
When we are one with our creator?
Once we reverse the fall
And return to our greatness?
The nature of nature is oneness
Lovingkindness atoned and humble
Wrapped in a quantum embrace
Infinite and eternal abundance
Connection that transcends the senses
No separation means no need for defenses
Togetherness until self defies mention
Release knowing into animated suspension
Love your enemies means have no enemies
Freedom for intuition to become preeminent
Brains kneel to hearts in reverence
'Til we know only love in spite of the evidence...
The nature of nature is evolution
A grand play of glorification
The chaos has an organization
And three parts to its constitution

Love and force and intelligence
Nothing is done for the hell of it
Heaven is always in the making
God spews truth without reticence
Intelligence and love and force
An upward momentum - a divine course
A flow to the energy of the universe
A purpose as defined by Source
Force and intelligence and love
The spirit represented by the dove
Holy and holistic part of a whole
Here I AM below as I AM above.

knowing where to look

If you are co-creating with intentional love, you are engaged in something true. The fabric of the cosmos is at your behest. Such is the nature of nature. You will be working with the flourishing current of a massive river. You will be plugging your blessings into the powerful conduit that is creation energy. When you have an idea in love, God will support your loving intentions with His own nature. Faith in that idea will move mountains. What is a mountain to God but a simple idea that can be simply adjusted? Nothing stands in the way of love that cannot be reduced to dust.

A miracle is no magnificent feat for God.

A miracle can be an idea that you share with God. It can be a perspective shift from yours to His. It can be an act in defiance of evil. It can be the leap of faith off of a cliff, an act of surrender, into the flourishing river.

On many occasions, I have given decisions over to God. In the midst of prayer, I have asked for guidance. At times his instruction has been subtle, written in His loving language. Other times he has spoken to me in beauty, for God knows that beauty truly is in the eye of the beholder. He can guide me with a special, well-placed brushstroke that would escape everyone else's attention but mine. Occasionally he speaks through humor. Laughter definitely is some of God's preferred medicine. Sometimes, though less frequently, He has cast aside the subtleties and has spoken bluntly.

I was in Colorado visiting a girl, and God spoke to me clearly.

the blue handsaw

For a couple months before Covid-19 holed us up in our houses, three of us began meeting weekly to discuss our fiction novels. It was Dillon, Bella the Coloradoan, and me. Our simple writing accountability group put a lot of momentum behind our books and our friendships. Occasionally, smaller groups would fracture off when all three of us could not meet. When the pandemic, Bella and I found ourselves having more and more *unofficial* meetings, talking less about our books and more about each other. As is often the case with me and girls I end up interested in, mere friendship held its form like a flooded balloon. One morning I woke up and the skin of our friendship had popped. I could think of little else besides talking to her, being with her.

So, in August of 2020, I planned a road trip from Austin to go see her in Colorado Springs.

While I was out there, a couple projects were on my mind. My fiction novel, of course. But also, Bella had just introduced me to the TV show *"Minimalists"*. The minimalist life appealed to me after spending a year living in my van, but I did not want to repeat adventures of the past. I was trying to sell my van, and I intended to use the earnings to begin work on a tiny home.

I told Bella I had become fully infected with Builder's Itch. She coyly suggested I build her a wooden frame for a beautiful painting she had been given by her brother. We went to Home Depot, got the wood, got the sandpaper, got the fasteners and picked out stain only to return home and realize I had no saw to cut the wood into shape.

I borrowed a blue handsaw from a neighbor and got to work. Within a matter of hours of building and a day of letting the stain dry, Bella the Coloradoan had her frame.

My feelings for her were deepening. I could still think of little else besides her. As my visit with her neared its end, there was a small denial of reality that it was then time to face. I lived in Austin and she lived in Colorado. Before she swept me off my feet, I had plunged my heart into the dream of building my tiny home. I was about to go home to Texas where I would begin construction. But that was so far away from this special girl. *Was there anything holding me in Texas, though? What if I could reimagine my grand plans somewhere in better proximity to Bella? I could build my tiny home in Colorado...*

The more I thought it through, the more my options became clear. If I moved to Colorado, I would first need to find a place to live. I would not ask Bella to be her roommate. Living with a significant other too early was not a smart option, I had learned. This meant that the tiny home would have to wait until I was settled in somewhere. But I would be in a state that I loved dearly, near a person I adored. If I went back to Texas, I would begin construction. I was set up well enough to begin immediately, but while I love Texas, it lacked a certain person.

Move or build. Those were my options.

One of my last mornings in Colorado, I took a walk with this prayer: " God, what do I do? *Do I move or build?*"

My walk turned into a wander. I followed my dog. He wanted to cross the street so we crossed the street. *"Move or build, God?"*

My dog continued to lead. *"Move or build?"*

And then, smack in the middle of the sidewalk, completely out of place, was a blue handsaw. It was the same model as the one I had just borrowed to *build* Bella her frame.

The message was clear: *Build.*

The next day, I drove back to Texas. Once back, I put an ad up on Craigslist looking for a garage that I could rent to build the tiny home. Skeeter responded immediately saying, "If you help me move some stuff out, you can use my garage for free." His garage was actually an air conditioned warehouse, with bay doors precisely the size that I needed. Skeeter and I shook hands and the project was underway.

Shortly thereafter, Bella came down to visit me in Austin. We had a great time. She fell in love with the city, and I fell in love with her. Without further ado, she began making arrangements to move to Texas. It was several long, challenging months before her lease was up in Colorado Springs, but ended up moving fifteen minutes from where I happily build.

I believe in a God who knows me. The religiosity that surrounds talk of God dampens the true nature of how I interact with Him. He and I have a *relationship*. His relationship with me is unlike His relationship with anyone else. Just as no two friendships are alike in our own lives, no two relationships are alike with God.

For anyone else, the handsaw on the sidewalk is meaningless. "Someone accidentally left their hand saw out," another would think. You might have thought that when you got to that point in the story. But God knows me. He knows how to meet me at my precise level of awareness. It is easy to write moments like this off as coincidence, or even superstition. We are all experiencing life from within ourselves, and that's where God speaks.

I told my mentor about the handsaw later that day. Saying it out loud made me feel vulnerable. As I was telling the story, I found myself tempering my conviction with, "I know it seems crazy to make a big life decision on something like that..."

"Not to me," he said. "God knows us perfectly."

We do not see with our eyes, we see through our eyes with our minds. God knows me, which means he knows my mind. When He puts things in my path, He knows that meaning - like beauty - is in the eye of the beholder. God would know that a blue handsaw, after using one a few days earlier to build, in the midst of prayer, setdown in the middle of my path no less, would elicit a reaction. And it did. It is still up to me to choose to listen to Him, but because I believe there is a lot more unknown to man than is known to man, I manage to maintain the belief that God works in ways mysterious to me. I do not have to lean on my own understanding. Why would I? I understand so little.

If you are still camping with the Seeing is Believing people, I hope the shortcuts discussed will help you see. I hope it will encourage you to keep an eye out for Him. The more you believe in His benevolent absurdity, the more synchronicities you will encounter. The more we strip God of His religious pretenses and come to know Him as an indwelling partner, a constant counselor, a highest intuition, an advocate, a comforter, an intercessor, a shared part of our consciousness grounded in goodness, the more we will see that He can only meet us at our current level of awareness. When our doting Father plays catch with us, he plays at our skill level. The curtain of separation was torn in twain. He is here, now. Begin to see Him and begin to believe. If you already have belief, then seeing will make your belief inexorable.

Without belief, you are left alone with your disbelief. Disbelief is a position on the edge of the chasm, where little can be heard over the echoing agony of lost souls.

Belief makes it real for you. Belief is the opening of your mind, and thus your eyes. Belief is the allowance of your awareness to expand. Belief is the welcoming of surrender. Belief is the first step on your divine journey.

You have a choice: You can believe in the permanent things that God will champion, or the temporary illusions that are moments from being washed away.

What will you choose?

the road to permanence part 2/4

Apenimon always showed up early for work in the lumberyard.

He was greeted by a few of the staff, while a few others withheld handshakes and avoided eye contact. He was used to the ethnic slurs. He had learned to ignore them when they were directed at him. He had more difficulty not standing up for his brothers and sisters, but when he did, he did so in a way that showcased his peoples' natural peacefulness. He realized long ago that he would not prove anyone wrong by proving them right.

In his role in the lumberyard, he spent much of his day working around machines, buzzsaws, and other high-energy equipment. The work environment was intense and cacophonous.

Apenimon found he was much more tolerant of ignorance before work than after. It was like he became as wound up as the machines. Slowly, throughout the day, his peaceful demeanor would be acclimated to the energy of his workplace. He could feel himself being infused with the disharmony. He much preferred work outside, in nature, or at worksites, but he did his best to decompress after work, knowing that if he worked hard this setting was temporary. But even so, he did not like the way he felt and was mindful to not let his frustration get the best of him.

One day, however, he found himself reacting instead of responding. At the end of the day, he was coated in sawdust. At some point, a wood shaving had leapt off the saw and cut his cheek. Without realizing it, he had smeared blood on the side of his face, like warpaint.

"You look so *brave* today, Apenimon!" his colleague mocked, changing his body language to that of a warrior. His tormentor and his cronies stood in a line, three of them, chanting in a musical fashion, *"Hi, how are ya?* Hi, how are ya? *Hi, how are ya?"*

Apenimon bumped into one of the cronies as he tried to get back. The man, in a flourish, threw himself down to the ground, yelping. The two others went along with the charade, pointing aghast at Apenimon, making a scene. "You savage!" one of them chided.

The hardworking, honest, and peaceful man raced out of the warehouse before anything more could come of it. Before driving home, he took a long walk. He knew their taunts had gotten the best of him, and he usually restrained himself much better. On his walk, he considered that maybe he was not cut out for this type of work. It was not putting him in the best mental state. Upon his return, the boss was waiting for him in the parking lot, standing akimbo. He gulped.

"Apenimon," he greeted with a firm handshake. "I notice you often take walks after work."

"Yessir," Apenimon said. "It helps me decompress."

The boss nodded thoughtfully. "I am aware that something happened this afternoon"

"I am sorry, sir," Apenimon said.

"Don't be. You put up with a lot from those guys, don't you?"

Apenimon had a well of frustration he wanted to let out. "I just wish for an opportunity to get to know each other better. I cannot understand why they are unable to see past their prejudices? They are hurtful. They are small-minded. It is frustrating, sir. Nothing I cannot handle, however."

"I completely agree, Apenimon. I believe there is very little you cannot handle. Which is why I am giving you a promotion."

"A promotion?" Apenimon tempered his excitement. He had come to the conclusion that he could not work in the loud, dark, cacophonous sawmill. He was prepared to be reassigned, and a promotion might not allow that. "What did you have in mind, sir?"

"Well, we're going to be doing a bit of restructuring. I lost three employees to our competitor just now. It's the three you are probably thinking of. I've come to the conclusion that our company is better off having them working for our competition. Do you agree?"

Apenimon held back a smile at his boss's cleverness. "You mean to say that, *coincidentally*, those three guys had offers from our competitor and today they decided to take them up?"

His boss smiled wide. "Yes. *Coincidentally*."

"I am sure you had nothing to do with that, sir."

"I may have given them the necessary push out the door," the boss said. "Which leaves a supervisory position open. It is kind of a mix of sales and support, actually. You would be driving to the various worksites where we supply, making sure the customers have everything they need. You would be spending a lot more time away from the lumberyard. Is that suitable? We need an honest, personable, and well-tempered man for the job. What do you say?"

Apenimon extended his hand to be shaken. "I'll take it."

There is no such thing as a neutral environment.

You are either filling yourself with life-giving power or being diminished. Your environment, or your collective diet, consists of anything and everything that you expose yourself to. This could be food and drink, but it also includes what you watch, listen to, think about, believe in, and surround yourself with.

Like the water examples discussed earlier in this chapter, humans are vibrationally impressionable. At the end of a long day in the city, immersed in the vibrations of steel, traffic, honking horns, anxious people, 5G, and bluetooth, I feel out of whack. Rather than rely on thinking or breathing my way out of my disarray, like trying to towel off while I am still in the noxious water, I change my environment.

The resonant frequency of Earth is within a couple Hertz of the resonant frequency of humankind. Whenever possible, I dive into nature and slip into natural, flowing water. The water acts like a conductor, completing the circuit between earth and myself. It is quickly recentering.

Resonant Frequencies:
Human Beings - around 7Hz
Earth / The Schumann Resonance - 7.83Hz
Cat's Meow - 25-150Hz
Dog Barking - 1000 - 2000Hz
Engine Noise - 1000 - 4000Hz
Bird Song - 1000 - 8000Hz
Dog Whistle - 35,000Hz
5G - 600MHz - 40GHz

You can download an audio frequency analyzer with a good quality microphone in order to find various resonant frequencies on your own. The human ear can hear between 20 - 20,000Hz. Quite often we go earblind to the cacophony around us. Quiet time and a stillness practice is paramount to the proper human function. Just as Apenimon could not find himself as easily after a day working in the mill, the same happens for us, sometimes imperceptibly.

IF YOU WANT TO TAKE YOUR INNER STATE SERIOUSLY, GO TO MATTHEWEMMOREY.COM/ COLLIDEOSCOPE AND DOWNLOAD A FREE COPY OF THE COLLIDE-O-SCOPE. THIS GAME PROVIDES 14 EXERCISES TO HELP YOU BECOME MORE AWARE OF THE EFFECTS OF YOUR LOCAL ENVIRONMENT.

Knowing that I am magnetic, I take my inner state seriously.

You cannot walk through life without changing the world around you. You will always attract more of what you are. This is why people who walk around angrily are significantly more likely to be attacked. Your vibration is so strong and impactful that the world mirrors you. Specific information is communicated within this energy. Because of the lag between belief and materialization, what you are receiving in your life is a reflection of what you had been exuding in your near past. In order to change what you are receiving, you must change what you are exuding. In other words, you can attune your electromagnetism to attract whatever you want more of. If you are conducting loving energy with loving thoughts, the matter around you will meet you where you are. The water you drink will be energized with love. Of course the opposite is also true. This is an art unto itself.

To make this sound less woo, let's use an aspiring musician as an example. The musician loves music. They love playing music, they love listening to music, they love talking about music. In most forms, it is *music to their ears*. Anyday this musician has some exposure to music, they are going to be in a better mood, exuding a much more pleasant energy, or at the very least, more attuned to the style of music they prefer. In the enjoyment of the beauty of music, their inner state becomes beauty. Inwardly and outwardly, they become more beautiful. In a way that has little to do with their physical appearance, the world around them absorbs and reflects their beauty.

This is the essence of the law of attraction. This is not something to be diminished into parlor tricks for attracting dates. This is a fundamental truth. Humans are vibrational beings. The world is a vibrational entity. Everything within the world has its own vibrational signature. Like attracts like. A round peg seeks a round hole.

Let's say you want to attract more money. You have the bright idea to stop paying for something that has previously cost you money, by *stealing* it. In your elementary mind, this is simple math. You will now have something that has value and you're not paying for it anymore. You have money and you also have the stuff. More money, right?

However, you are a vibrational being. Paying full price for something communicates to your subconscious - and thereby your energy - that you can afford it. You have the added benefit of truth and honesty interwoven into your being. You can stand a little taller, convey a bit more presence, believe in your ability to afford things. By spending, you are attuning your vibration to more. The world responds in kind by "*trusting*" you with more resources. More importantly, your actions reflect a deep belief in your own trustworthiness. You are not trying to cheat the system, you are not a cheat, but someone who will responsibly marshal the resources that flow through you.

MATTHEW 5:15 READS,

"Nor would someone light a lamp and then put it under a basket; rather, it is placed upon a lampstand so that it may afford light to all in the house."

It is the most natural behavior of the one infused with light, to shine.

On the flip side, if you apply the original strategy, you convey to your subconscious that you have to steal to live a certain lifestyle. You tell the universe that you are going to play by different rules. You will sneak around in stealth in order to get more for less. You shrink, and your vibration lowers. The universe responds in kind by aligning its blessings for you with you, thereby "*trusting*" you with less. Before long, you can no longer afford what you once could. Deceit does not work on the universe. It is a poor long-term strategy. Humans can be easily tricked - take Adam and Eve in the garden of Eden - but the universe is untrickable. The law of attraction never takes breaks.

Rest assured that the punishment one is owed by robbing or thieving will not only be waiting in the afterlife. They are systematically attuning themselves to squalor. Even if the most apt measuring stick of their squalor is not financial, rest assured there are fruits they will never know the sweetness of, that an honest person enjoys on the daily. *They have no idea what they are missing.*

This is all a matter of alignment. The law of attraction works by giving you what you are in alignment with. The world does not define stuff the way we do. What we think of as magnificent is just another vibration to the universe.

raising your vibrational signature

In 2019, one of my friends made less than $10,000 in the entire year. Toward the end of 2019, this friend began studying the law of attraction and applying it into her life. This friend was committed to feeling deeply into herself, transmuting the things that kept returning her to low vibrational states like bitterness and anger. She repaired relationships with estranged family members, she learned how to ask for help, she poured herself into her work. It was no easy task for her. Quite often throughout the first half of 2020, her pendulum swung out of balance and she found herself with new issues to resolve. But overtime, with commitment, by paying full price for life coaches and courses, by blooming wherever she was planted, by standing a little taller and a little more confidently, by saying yes to the challenges that came her way, by taking radical responsibility for her beliefs and her thoughts, by maintaining a nutritious diet, a healthy gut and a diligent fitness regimen, she elevated her alignment to an unprecedented level. At the end of 2020, her new company owed her over $2 million dollars.

You could look at this as God prospering her. Certainly her relationship with Him improved as she spent more time in love. The more time she spent in communion with the Lord, the more playful and childlike she was, as anyone who is doted on by a loving Father becomes. However, I believe that her income was not God choosing to reward her. His love and the jubilation of His fruits is His reward. The rekindled relationship with her family members is His reward...

The money is just the universe's response to her quantum leap. The universe is not a doting Father, like God is. Money is not God's reward. The fruits of the spirit are God's reward; things like love, joy, peace, patience, kindness, goodness, faithfulness, gentleness and temperance. These are a wealth of another kind. The money came because the universe was doing what it does - responding. There is a reason why the universe did not rise up to block this quantum leap, but instead simply responded as responsibility and reliably as always. There is no law that says someone cannot 2000x their income year over year. There is no law that says someone's vibrational alignment can only change so much. You can choose whatever alignment you wish, and the universe will respond. It is completely and utterly indifferent. There are no degrees of magnitude. The universe is like a vending machine. You input your vibrational selection and it gives you what you ordered. The vending machine does not judge your selection. It just does what it was programmed to do.

If you put out low vibrations with thoughts about hatred and rage, the universe will not be disappointed in you. It has no expectations. It is completely indifferent. When you reach into the vending machine's slot to retrieve its response and you are bit by a snake, you are not being punished. The universe is merely aligning. The response you welcome is not a pat on the back or a "*good job*", though you can choose to view it that way as a barometer of your alignment with what you desire. You may use these responses gratefully as guides in the direction of your highest alignment. **You may conveniently find that the closer you align with God, with love, with joy and play, with trust and abundance, the easier it becomes to receive what you desire most.**

It is important to know that God would have loved my friend just the same had she made another $10,000 in 2020. The universe's responses are not dictations of your worth or inherent value. The universe is helpless to respond in kind - it must.

There are basically two things at work here. First, and most importantly, in applying biblical teachings, she sought a proximity to the Father. The stronger their relationship became, the easier it was for her to attune her vibration to material abundance. One's relationship with God is rewarded with spiritual blessings that tend to unblock potential material manifestations. For example, if you are in a sales profession and a potential customer is wanting to choose between two companies with comparable products, being a channel of love, joy, peace, patience, kindness and goodness will likely sway their decision. Remember, we are not alone in the experience of our vibration. Would you rather work with someone who makes you feel like family or just another number?

IT IS WRITTEN IN MATTHEW:

> "So if you are offering your gift at the altar and there remember that your brother has something against you, leave your gift there before the altar. First go and be reconciled to your brother; then come and offer your gift."

If one did not follow this biblical teaching, they would go about their life with anger toward their family, unreconciled. All it might take is the sight of two siblings lovingly conversing in the grocery store to be triggered out of your fruitful state. Suddenly you are angry, you take a step back from God, and also fall out of alignment with your abundance. The altar is *internal*, our relationship with love is within us, and we cannot fully be that love while seeds of bitterness grow within us.

One's relationship with God comes first. Always. Worship the King whose kingdom is in Heaven. Once that relationship is strong and intimate, you can further attune yourself to earthly things.

C.S. Lewis said, "If you aim at heaven you will get Earth thrown in. If you aim at Earth, you will end up with neither."

I believe in God and I see the truth in the law of attraction. I know Him and I feel It. They are both real and true. One is so loving and attentive, while the other is so matter-of-fact and indifferent. The universe is not the one conspiring in your favor. The universe does not care about you or the sparrows. God does. The reason God comes first is because He is the active, attentive One. God is into growing His children. He knows us so intimately. He always knows what we desire, and when those desires are godly, He always knows what we need to get in alignment with them. Therefore, He is constantly orchestrating circumstances for the benefit of our evolution. God wants us at His side, standing with poise, presence, posture; self-actualized. He wants us to become who He has imagined us to be.

There are things at this moment that are out of my vibrational reach. I have my upbringing, conditioning and my programming, just the same as everyone else. I have unconscious stories, a sin-nature, and a largely-undeveloped-yet-developing world view. There are still plenty of blessings that I am blocking. With His help, immersed into the Father-childlike relationship that He offers me, I stand a chance of walking with the level of trust necessary to reach my potential. I cannot do it on my own. Only by knowing Him, by knowing how much He loves me, by knowing how adamant He is about delivering me to situations to overcome my shallowness, and only by knowing that He has allowed or orchestrated the challenges in my life for my benefit - in past, present, and future - do I get to stand in the belief that I will arrive at the magnificence that He has imagined for me.

This is the mentality of *The Detourist.*

This calls for both surrender and ownership.

surrender

Twins, Amy and Brenda, want nothing more than peace. They have lived difficult lives, narrowly avoiding the many pitfalls their childhood has presented them. Now, the faults of their upbringing are beginning to show psychological effects. Anxiety, depression, and chronic stress plague their every decision.

Amy tells herself that she is okay, but she is not. The little girl who was once so free and authentic is no more. Each day she goes to bed with slightly less enthusiasm. She dreams of peace, but cannot see a path from Here to There.

Brenda surrenders. She confesses her issues. She decides because her struggles are putting her dreams on hold anyway that she will take some time to address the causes of them. She easily identifies a childhood that distanced her from herself. She dreams of peace. She knows it will not be easy, but she is determined to get there.

Amy and Brenda are equally capable but before long, Brenda begins to get ahead. When triggering challenges emerge, Amy seeks peace. She finds scraps of peace moments after chastising the person, situation, or circumstance that triggered her. She samples peace the second after she places blame. She feels the most peace when she is alone, so consciously or not, she pushes anything that could disrupt her peace away.

Brenda handles her triggers differently. Brenda recognizes that anything with the power to disrupt her peace owns a part of her. She is eager to take herself back. When a challenge triggers an unsavory emotion, Brenda asks, 'Why am I having such a strong reaction to this?' Her curiosity leads to discussion with professionals. She learns about coping mechanisms, patterns, and conditioning. She identifies a helpful, if not irritating, part of herself that is constantly fixated on protecting her - her ego. Nothing about this process is peaceful for Brenda, but she trudges forward. She seeks a lasting peace. She knows that true peace will be surrendering to her reality, accepting the facts, and acting accordingly.

Amy's desire for peace now prevents her from recognizing the truth. The poor girl believes that if she admits her sadness, the pain will overwhelm her. So, she maintains her rigidity. She closes her heart and does what she needs to do to get through the day. Her lack of progress, her blame game, and her victim mentality eventually threads itself into her identity. It becomes something she cannot grow out of. Amy believes that she is broken. Unfixable. Ugliness is no longer merely her transitory condition, but in Amy's mind, it is who and what she is.

Meanwhile, Brenda does not identify with her issues. Brenda addresses them. Brenda brings her pain to the light. It is not pretty, but in the light, it changes. The healing girl improves. She remembers comfort. She approaches peace.

Before long, Amy finds herself in a dark place. She is lonely. She tries to force connection but her energy is abrasive. She becomes harsh. She does not know peace because she is not an instrument of peace. Wishing people were different does not make them different. Everyone around her disappoints her. Nobody ever sticks around. In Amy's experience, people suck. People have always sucked.

On the contrary, everywhere Brenda goes, there is peace. Peace envelops her like an aura. Brenda was willing to surrender, to forego peace and embrace discomfort, and now she enjoys its lasting presence. In Brenda's experience, people are mirrors. She comes to love others, and enjoys a rich and healthy social life.

✦ ✦ ✦

the ease of life

Surrender is an important principle of the Detourist. It is about putting your relationship with Love first. If you try to attune yourself to the worldly abundance before attuning yourself to Love, you will be blocked. You will fall. You will have to effort your way through life, only to receive fractions of what you desire. You will be exhausted by this effort. You will tire, and you will watch the fruits that require your constant effort waste away. **Surrendering to how God wants to bring these blessings into your life is the only way.**

Surrender to Love.

Surrender to trust.

Surrender to truth.

In our masculinized society, we might find a quick rejection to the idea of surrender. There was never a war won by surrendering. In fact, surrendering is an act of submission, an acceptance of defeat.

If you did well, you *crushed* it. You wrecked your goals. You destroyed all projections. You smashed the competition. You killed it! You're a beast! You absolutely slayed. You're the bomb! You are a force to be reckoned with. You bad, king. You are deadly. You're a savage. What a *beast!*

As I write these, I actually begin to feel a sense of affirmation. I get a little hyped up. But the language is aggressive. This is what we are taught in the world. We end up revering physical strength and might, and scratch our heads at ideas like, "The meek shall inherit the Earth." And then we start missing "church" on Sunday because our football team is playing a noon game.

We wind up worshiping men and war-games, and we wonder why our values shift. (For the record, I love football. After worship.)

So surrender is not an obvious choice. If you are *of the world*, that is, unconsciously conformed to human defaults, you might wake up with the intention to conquer. To have your will be done. To beat back the competition to get yours. To win! Surrender is not on the menu. Let's go!

The idea is very appealing to my ego. I am super competitive...

This mentality is easy.

Surrender is hard. To view myself as separate and to beat back others is convenient. To only care about myself and my tribe is simple. To care little about understanding my enemy, to have enemies, takes no effort whatsoever. To view the world as black and white is effortless. It's so lazy that it literally takes no effort whatsoever.

It is the default. It is the road most frequently traveled.

To diverge is to take the Detour.

A prerequisite to surrender is knowing that the nature of nature is Love. The only shortcut from *Here* to *There* is Love. Competition is not a godly idea, cooperation is. If at the core of existence, nature was in competition with itself, then life would only have progressed to the point of battle-ready single-celled organisms. On life's more basic level, cells came together to unify and form more complex organisms.

Fast forward to today: your idea of you is an amalgamation of 30 trillion cells and 100 trillion microbes. You have given yourself a name and an identity, but basically, we are an illusion stitched together by memory.

Competition, the idea of being something separate, and the illusions made by our egos, do not make rational sense. Your ego tells you that you will die at the end of your life because your ego will die at the end of your life. If not sooner. You are not your ideas, nor are you your ego's ideas.

Surrender is merely aligning yourself with divinity. If you must give yourself an identity in this lifetime, identify with being human - which is in part, divine. This is one heck of a special privilege. The purpose in your being alive is to see God, to know God, and to love God. That is to say, you are here to learn and to be in Love. You will find Him inside yourself in various forms - in ideas like forgiveness, unity, peace, righteousness, beauty, or creativity. Surrender to that. Keep surrendering every day to that. Seek perfect surrender and your dreams will unfold naturally. While you are busy surrendering, He will be listening to your heart, the law of attraction will be working, and you will be able to stay out of your own way in manifesting your dreams.

One divine part of being human is our God-image, our imaginations. Humans use this gift by imagining our future. Together we shape what we are stepping into. Surrender to your highest ideals. Envision a fruitful and inclusive future. Notice the importance of trust in that vision. Then lead with trust.

My therapist often reminds me, "*Trust* but verify." You do not have to heedlessly make yourself vulnerable. Be thorough if that is what you need to begin trusting more deeply. Trust is a key ingredient in surrender, and a necessity for connecting with our fellow humans.

If you must be in competition with something, be against selfishness and shallowness. Be against the illusions of your ego. Your ego feeds on stories, drama, and ideas of self-importance. The vital ingredient in stories is time - past and future. A story cannot exist without time. Starve your ego by being here, now. If you surrender to the present moment in a state of love, time ceases to exist. Forgiveness dissolves the past. Surrender dissolves the barbs in the future. Unity dissolves a story's *other characters*. Beauty burns away distractions, leaving you here and now. Surrender to these things, and watch your ego wriggle and writhe as it begs for food. With practice, with determination, with groundedness, with God, you will evolve to be unaffected by your ego's dramatic hunger pangs. You can die to the idea of your vulnerable self well before your body dies, and live out your life unblocked by your shallow ideas.

Surrender to His greatness. Allow yourself to receive yours.

Surrender is merely trust. Perhaps you put that trust in Him. Perhaps you say, "No matter what happens, I will make the most of it." Or, "No matter what happens, I will be okay." From this place of peace, you are often much better than okay - even joyful.

Surrender is acceptance of an important fact. You are not in control. There are only three things you are truly in control of: your effort, your attitude, and your alignment. You can always do your best. You can always make the most of it. You can always surrender to a higher ideal. Whatever happens in your life can either be rejected or used for your highest good.

Part of the beauty of being human is choice. You are not in control of the circumstances, but you can choose how you respond. You can play a co-creation role in what comes next. If you are going through hell and you raise more, you also have to live in it.

Surrender is an act of keen awareness. It is recognizing the momentum behind the universe, and allowing it to move you. It is maintaining your alignment, but going with the flow. A friend of mine describes it like jet skiing. You have your own force, but it pales in comparison with the power of the ocean. If you put your force against the oceans, you will quickly be humbled. If you pair your momentum with the ocean, you are capable of magnificent things.

Try on some other affirmations that are more in alignment with surrender.

1. I will maintain my alignment regardless of the outcome.
2. What is meant for me can never pass me by.
3. With Him, all things are possible.
4. I can do all things through Christ who strengthens me.
5. I will ensure to nurture myself.
6. Life is long enough for me to be patient.
7. God has never removed anything from my life without replacing it with something better.
8. I am open to receiving.
9. Call my name and I will go.
10. I serve you, so let me understand your teachings.

11. This moment provides for me everything I need.
12. God does not implant a desire He does not intend to fulfill.

Surrender is no easy feat. It takes a lot of trust. In the beginning, surrender can feel like patience. The trouble with patience, however, is patience is a close relative of impatience. You might be patiently waiting for something, but you are still tacitly acknowledging a lack in your life. If you have surrendered completely, this moment is meeting you with everything you need. You are not dwelling in the past or the future, you are not comparing and contrasting your life with what could be, and most importantly, you are not lacking anything. *There is nothing to be patient about.* Surrender is a complete acceptance of where you are. It is a non-attachment to any particular outcome, while maintaining an assurance that your well-being state of mind will be accessible regardless of your circumstances. Patience, therefore, is a moot point. You know that God does not plant a desire in your heart that he does not intend to fulfill. It will be fulfilled. When it will be fulfilled is not your business, it's His. To be immersed in the present in appreciation of all that is creates *timelessness.*

This is the disposition of surrender: trusting nonchalance and overflowing appreciation of the here and now.

wants and desires

God plants desires in us.

A desire in your heart is a charge - a little love energy - stoking you in the direction of some action. You play with the energy of these desires, but you do not play with the attitude of lack. There is a stark difference between the *wants* in your life and the *desires*.

A wanting mind is not a surrendered mind. A wanting mind is not a mind at peace. It is incomplete without the thing it wants. A desiring mind can remain playful and surrendered, enjoying a completeness while charged with the energy of the object of desire.

Desire is an indication of love. Want is an indication of lack. If you have trouble differentiating between the two in this section, I invite you to think of desire as beauty. It is merely something that stokes the magic within you.

A wanting mind can quickly get stuck in the mud. It can want something so strongly that it focuses solely on the lack of it. That might be a want for perfection, a want for romance, a want for arrival, a want for external security.

If we *want* too much, we can begin to see only the lack in our lives, and not the blessings.

More times than once in my life, I have gotten stuck in the mud. I have not only *not surrendered*, but I have dug my heels in stubbornly, and refused to accept reality. I have been blinded by where I *want* to be, what I *want* to have, what I *want* to be true, or what I *want* to feel.

stuck in the mud

A woman jumps in her horse-drawn wagon and sets out for a destination. The journey is a couple hour ride, and she contents herself by thinking about her destination. "I can't wait to be there!" There are many pleasant attractions along the road, but she has no interest. She is distracted by her thoughts of arrival.

A couple hours into the journey, she checks her watch, thinking, "I should arrive at my destination soon!" A couple more hours later, she is getting confused. "This is a two hour ride," she thinks, "Why have I not arrived?"

There are still many pleasant distractions around her, but once again, she sinks into her distracted mind with thoughts of where she wants to be. As frustration begins to set in, she distances herself from her reality.

Not long after this initial frustration, a traveler meets her on the road. He approaches her, shouting, "Ma'am, do you need help?"

"No!" she answers. She is sure that she does not. Not to mention she is a little irritated that she has not arrived yet. "I'm fine!"

"You sure?" he asks again.

She does not respond. She returns to her stewing. "What a creep," she says.

Another couple hours go by. Now she has become aware that something is wrong. She still has not arrived at her destination, and the sun is beginning to set. There are birds chirping and pleasant distractions abound, but there is the clearness of a problem, too. Inside her wagon she considers herself and her destination. "I should be there by now," she grumbles.

Around dusk, she can no longer ignore the nagging sensation in her gut. "Why did that man ask me if I needed help? I'm fine." And then an attempt at an explanation for her gut feeling. "Sometimes things take longer than you expect. I don't have a problem..."

Just then, another traveler approaches her on the road. A man's voice says, "By golly, miss, you have gotten yourself deeply stuck in the mud."

"No, I have not," she answers stubbornly.

"You certainly have," he assures her.

"That's not possible," she answers. "Someone like me is too clever to get stuck in the mud. I would never let that happen. I am not that kind of person. If I was stuck in the mud, that would mean..." She starts unraveling a story in her head. The thought of not listening to her intuition, of being imperfect, of making a silly mistake, and then of denying her reality... "No, no," she rejects. The thoughts make her body feel poisoned! She hates the feeling! *Ick!* "I'm good, thank you very much," and she dismisses the traveler. She does her best to distance herself from those horrible sensations.

Hours go by.

And then days.

Finally, the truth begins to dawn on her. The simple mistake of getting stuck in the mud has been compounded by a much worse mistake: denial. In a burst of decisiveness, she looks down and sees the wheels of her wagon sunken into clumpy mud. Now in acceptance of her circumstances, she deals with her reality. She gets herself unstuck, and she continues on...

Alan Watts, in his book *The Wisdom of Insecurity* talks about how we want to predict our futures. If we know what is coming, we can be ready for it. So, instead of being in our present reality in as much understanding and acceptance of it as possible, we are somewhere else. We are in our minds immersed in a reimagined past or a concocted future. From this paranoid creation, this *illusion*, we build our best guess about where things are headed.

This would be like waking up in tropical paradise, but in your imagination you're in Michigan in January. You dress yourself in snow pants and winter gear and then step outside into 90 degree sunshine.

How are you going to predict your future from a present you are not present in? Better to be present and trusting, and take what cues the universe is giving you in the moment. The prediction of your life is futile, but at least you will be grounded enough to take the hints you are being given. The hints may be hard pills to swallow, but you are much better off acknowledging them.

The first step in getting unstuck is acknowledging that you are, in fact, stuck. Getting into a sticky situation is a natural part of getting out of your comfort zone. But getting stuck is often a symptom of not paying attention to what is true and right in front of you. The greatest obstacles to the present are the past and future. Adamantly clear them out of your view.

I recognize that this is easier said than done. Our whole lives can feel wrapped up in a single illusion. If we break the illusion, what else will crumble apart? The worry that accepting the truth will bring catastrophic ruin is a fallacy. Ease and effortlessness await the surrendered one. The phenomenon seems paradoxical, but actually, by admitting to yourself what is true, you give yourself an opportunity to address reality. Most problems have simpler fixes that we expect.

THE COMPANION TO THE DETOURIST, THE COLLIDE-O-SCOPE, IS ONE PATHWAY TO SURRENDER. IF YOU WOULD LIKE TO DO THE WORK BUT DO NOT KNOW EXACTLY HOW, GO TO WWW.MATTHEWEMMOREY.COM/COLLIDEOSCOPE FOR A FREE DOWNLOADABLE COPY.

nature + nurture

A familiar Elder Soul sits across a pond of light from me. Together, our consciousnesses bask in delightful comfort. Images swirl across the surface of the pond, and the Elder gestures toward them. "Here is the life you are preparing to live."

I look at the images, taking them in with great interest. I have been in this place before. Countless times this Elder and I have sat at this pond, but the feelings are always the same: nervousness, intrigue, inevitability.

The Elder patiently repeats a rehearsed speech. "Your purpose on Earth is evolution. Incarnation into humanity is school, my Soul. Eventually you will return to this realm and we will reflect upon what you learned, as we have before. Are you ready to become *Matthew?*"

"I am."

"Remember, within the womb, you experience a sort of amnesia. You will not remember me. Or this conversation, or this place, or this realm. You will forget in order to be fully appropriated into this body. At your Soul's level, you will ask questions such as *'Why am I here, in this body, on this planet?'* You will sense the immaterial like a phantom limb. The answer to that question is simple: You go to see, know, and to love God. You go to be in service. There are other parts of the Oneness who are hurt, and are hurting others. You go to help them heal, so they may see, know, and love God, as well. Do you still wish to make this choice?"

"I do."

"You won't remember making this choice. You will start out believing you are this human and nothing more. With time, you may begin to remember the truth, that you chose the trials that await you not to be overcome by them, but to assume your true nature through them. All of them are to aid your evolution. There will be plenty. You will meet all of them as you are, and as such, each and every one will be an opportunity. There will be no accidents, no coincidences, no random happenstance so long as you understand that God is with you every step. It will be a great challenge to avoid being distracted by the temptation to define your circumstances, my Soul. You will see that humanity's view of God will differ based on each person's level of consciousness. God will remain the power of life, but these temptations may lead you to define Him based on your interpretations. Can you understand what I am saying?"

"I can."

"*Learning is everywhere.* You are the vessel. You will be the Giver of Meaning for yourself. If you can remember that you have chosen all of this for the sake of your evolution, then the meaning you give will be eternal and infinite. When you succumb to the most common temptation of mankind, when you avoid learning, the trial will repeat itself. You can learn on the first trial, or the trial can repeat endlessly until you learn."

The Elder continued, "Some of the trials are related to generational curses. You are inheriting these from your ancestors. Some of the trials will be self-inflicted. You are going to start out as a baby who is inexperienced coping in this world. You will not always act gracefully. You will be raised by parents with trials of their own. While nobody can complete the trial of another, your dynamic with your parents can be for the highest evolution for you all. And lastly, some of the trials are for humanity. For a return to divinity, to Love; a reversal of the Fall that created the illusion of separation. God is inevitable, my Soul."

"It's kind of ironic, isn't it? I am going to be incarnated in a world of individuals with the goal of helping them remember their unity."

"*Re-member*. That's a perfect word for it. You may also become *of the world*, which is to say, you may embody the energies of the one who kills and destroys. His force is great, and many are in his grip. You may learn and adopt his ways, in emotions like hatred and despair, or shame and guilt. There is always a chance we end up back here, sooner than we should, discussing how your existence led to apathy. I believe your Soul has arrived at a groundedness in our Father's glorious power, however, and should you continue to remember Him, this destroying force will gain no purchase on your Soul. Do you understand?"

"I understand."

"Are you ready?"

And then the lessons began.

✦   ✦   ✦

Nature vs. Nurture and nature vs. nurture are two similar conversations with vastly different scales.

The nature versus nurture conversation takes into account what we get from our parents and ancestors, and then how we integrate into our world. There is a long list of things from generational curses to childhood traumas to address. There are also generational blessings and imbued passions to celebrate. We tend to get too serious about our evolution sometimes...

reunion

My Uncle Mark works for the U.S. Fish and Wildlife Service. The Agency manages National wildlife refuges, protects endangered species, manages migratory birds, restores nationally significant fisheries and enforces federal wildlife laws, distributes funds for wildlife conservation to states and territories, regulates international wildlife trade, and makes many other conservation efforts.

When my Uncle Mark was transferred from a small town in South Dakota to a smaller town in Idaho, he was venturing out into parts unknown for members of our family.

One day he was walking through the aisles of the small grocer in Orofino, Idaho when he heard his father's laugh. Anyone who knows Dr. Ed Drobish knows that laugh. It is loud and boisterous. It is the kind of laugh that brings everyone in the vicinity in on the joke. But Uncle Mark's dad was 2,000 miles away in Michigan. Even so he poked his head into the next aisle to see. Standing in the aisle was a man of similar build to my grandfather, who also shared his most prominent attribute: a large, Ukrainian nose.

My uncle approached under the guise of the friendly newbie in town. He said, "My name is Mark Drobish. I just moved to town..."

The laughing man looked him up and down and said, "My name is Stan Drobish." Stan is a cousin of my grandfather, and until that moment, those two sides of our family were estranged.

Amongst the many generational blessings I have been given is a quickness of laughter. Laughter is one of the primary ways I find my own tribe, and sometimes it helps our family find each other in unsuspecting places like Orofino, Idaho.

It seems that my family tree is being sculpted with many duplicate parts. Some of us have the same nose, laugh, body shape, hair color, or eye color. Members of both sides of my family seem to be passing down a stubborn disposition. This stubbornness could very well lead us to immovable shallowness. Or it might couple well with the value of hard work that was demonstrated for me by my parents growing up.

This commitment to hard work may lead to a need to regain work life balance. Fortunately, growing up, my dad was often around. He coached all of my sports. I watched him turn down promotions to spend more time with us. When I stubbornly plunge into professional ambitions to a depth where I begin sacrificing family, I need only remember the model I have in my dad. My family shares a lot of things. We can easily relate to each other on various levels. We share our looks, and many other things that are not so pretty. My dad and I are simultaneously transcending a hubris that got us both fired from long-standing jobs.

In the future, there will be trials that I cannot yet foresee, but I will not be alone. I hope the lessons I learn from my future trials will provide models for my family to transcend other generational hardships, as my dad has done so richly for me.

I say this to illustrate the process of our evolution. A family has *inevitabilities*. Generational curses are inevitably going to show up in a new member's life. Nobody has cracked the code yet. Some of them *really* want to. However, your evolution may terrify or depress others.

Denzel Washington said, "Your own family will talk shit about you when you're in the process of breaking generational curses. This ain't for the weak."

These inevitabilities are like the snares used for trapping animals. You can be going about your life, minding your own business, when you get snared into the trap. The only way out of this trap, oftentimes, is to mangle yourself in the process of escaping. It might happen a thousand times before you learn how to avoid it. It will keep happening until you figure it out.

THIS IS WHAT WE ARE HERE FOR, TO ADDRESS THE CONDITIONS THAT CAUSE US TO CLOSE OUR HEARTS. IN DOING SO, WE HAND THE REVELATIONS UP AND DOWN OUR LINEAGE. IN THE SUBSEQUENT CHAPTERS, AND WITHIN THE COLLIDE-O-SCOPE, WE ANALYZE OUR SNARES AND IDENTIFY HOW TO LEARN WHAT THEY ARE THERE TO TEACH US. BY SEEKING THE LOVING SOLUTION, THROUGH SURRENDER, BY ADOPTING A SPIRIT OF PLAY, AND A FEW OTHER WAYS, WE STAND A CHANCE TO ACCOMPLISH THE EVOLUTION THAT WE CAME FOR.

TO GET A FREE COPY OF THE COLLIDE-O-SCOPE WHICH WILL HELP IDENTIFY SOME KEY AREAS FOR YOUR GROWTH, GO TO WWW.MATTHEWEMMOREY.COM/COLLIDEOSCOPE.

The snare is essentially part of your shape. It is one of those duplicate parts that gets passed down to children. If your parents never figured it out and you have not either, your child will certainly inherit the opportunities to do so. For the sake of evolution. None of these *snares* are intended by God to keep you down. They are merely part of reversing the Fall. It is not your fault that you or your parents inherited them, but it is completely your responsibility to address them now.

Why so serious? Remember, you have also been given an arsenal of generation weaponry.

In essence, the nature versus nurture conversation *is* the same as the Nature versus Nurture conversation. If nature is what you get from your ancestors, then Nature is what God has imagined you to be on a spiritual level. If nurture is how you integrate into the world throughout your life, then Nurture is the means by which God will help you self-actualize into His highest idea of you. He is with you every step of the way.

You are not doing this work for yourself alone. Immediately, you are doing it for your family.

Mother Theresa said, "The problem is we draw the circle of our family too small."

Eventually, you are doing it for humankind. Inevitably, though, life will be lived in union with the Loving Mind. Innocence cannot project, and from a state of innocence all you will be able to create is love.

CHAPTER 1.5

play

As children, my playmates and I were always elsewhere. The backyard became a battlefield. The blanket fort became a castle. As we aged, our vision matured in a variety of ways. The abandoned house on the corner became a murder scene. The man who walked his dog slowly around the neighborhood was a zombie or an arsonist or the man behind the murders at the corner house! Whatever suited our imaginations, unencumbered by "practicality", became our reality. And we lived in it. We floated in make-believe until our moms called us in for dinner. And there we wolfed down our food so we could finish our mission. Nowadays, my best friends use their vision to write bestselling novels, run multimillion dollar companies, or simply play Dungeons and Dragons.

We were living inside our own imaginations. We still are. We are creative people.

In my day job, I helped people write books. I am an author, motivator, and coach, of sorts. One question I often ask people is, "What makes you want to write a book?" Quite often, with emotion in their voices, people answer," *I am such a creative person!*"

I love that answer. However, that answer is no different from saying, "I am a human being!" You are a creative person. We all are creative people. Even the most pragmatic person I know is actively creating the lifestyle he desires for his family. *Everybody dreams.* We were created in God's image, remember? That line alone tells you everything you need to know. The Creative Power that created us made us like Him.

Some of us are more inclined toward imagination than others. Children, for example, are expert players. When I play with my nieces, it is imaginative exercise. One moment I am playing a bear and they are playing cubs, and the next moment I am playing an avalanche sweeping down a mountain or a flood breaking through a dam as I chase them around the yard. These are perfectly acceptable games to a child. These are games ripe with imagination. Sometimes, as I scoop up my niece and we tumble about on the grass, I see in her eyes that she believes she is in an actual avalanche. It is real to her, and she is terrified. *Whoops,* I went too hard into character.

Who is more creative and imaginative than a child? They look around their world with vision and never stop to doubt their creativity. What if we grew up and maintained that authority? There are very few differences between the wild dreamer and the playful child. The most potent imagineers I know have grown up to be CEOs with strong visions, novelists, actors, mentors, coaches, and musicians. These people have maintained their imaginations into adulthood, and continued to playfully reinvent themselves.

Alan Watts said, "The secret to life is being in the here and now and realizing it is not work, it is play."

A lot of people are after passive income in their life. They crave leisure and the necessary income to finance it. We work so hard at our jobs to take a week or two week vacation, and then we get back to work. At times, I have been guilty of working a passionless job so I had money for escapes like this. The vacations from this type of work satiate my desire for leisure, but they are largely unfulfilling.

To borrow fragments from James Michener, a *Detourist* makes little distinction between their work and their play, their labor and their leisure, their mind and their body, their education and their recreation, their love and their religion. The *Detourist* hardly knows which is which. They simply pursue a vision of excellence at whatever they do, leaving others to decide whether they are working or playing. To them, they are always doing both.

The cycle between effort and sloth leaves much to be wanted. It leaves me starving for more time to pursue my passions. But I don't pursue them. I lack the time or the energy. This lifestyle slowly and imperceptibly subtracts the passion from your life. *All work and no play makes Jack a dull boy.* Jack is a depressed boy, too.

Jim Carrey says depression is your body telling you it's sick of playing the character you are pretending to be. Nobody is put on this planet to work. That the soil requires tilling is a consequence of our condition. Work is not meant to be our purpose. If we make *work* the purpose of our character, that character is going to get sick pretty quickly. Jim Carrey is the perfect person to teach us about playing characters. What he understands is that nobody else can force you into a certain shape by deciding that is who you are. Perhaps that is who you were, but we are supposed to change.

Life seems to be a process of remembering. Remembering who and what we are, remembering where we came from, re-*membering* to the body of love. The more we remember, the easier it is to slip out of the expectations and pressures of others, and into the selves that come most naturally. The easier it is to take the Detour when all other paths and the momentum of others seem to only point one way.

The world is our stage, we are characters, and life unfolds like a great play.

Already, the play has proven to be magnificent. These types of things only come in two categories: *tragedy* or *comedy*. This play is not a tragedy. From inside it, we experience tragic things - some in reality and some in our perception - but this is a comedy. Beauty can come out of something tragic, and tragedy is never the final act. Comedy has the upper hand. Have you ever had such a long series of misfortune mark your bad day that suddenly, out of the blue, it becomes hilarious? Comedy has a way of showing up in the minds of characters, and how can there be tragedy while there is laughter? Comedy is a sneaking trickster. It's always lurking, waiting for the opportunity to laugh with you. Tragedy exists, in small snippets and in narrow perspectives, but comedy is the throughline of the story. Tragedy might win the day, but comedy wins the life.

How do you live differently if you are stepping onto the stage of a comedy? How do you play differently? How do you work differently, so that it ceases to be work? And if your work became play, would you *work* another day in your life?

Passive income is generally viewed as income that is generated by work done in the past. That is one definition. However, if you were to play all day, and that play happened to earn you money, that is also passive income. Non-passive income is money you have to make an effort for. It's labor. It's work. The passionless job and escapist vacation is a worker's lifestyle. Imagine for a moment that you had all the money that you could ever need. Would you imitate what the escapist does on vacation for the rest of your life? Or two weeks into this indulgent lifestyle, would you find it mundane and meaningless? How long could you sit on your ass doing nothing before you went crazy?

About three days for me.

If I had all the money I could ever need, I would do things. I would do exactly what I wanted to do. I would challenge myself, I would learn, I would take on interesting projects, and I would immerse myself into my interests. Because I am doing these things out of pure enjoyment, I would do them thoroughly and well. There is a good chance some of those endeavors would go on to earn me money. Does this income change my profitable activities into work? No. This is more passive income.

Take J.K. Rowling for example. If she set out to write the Harry Potter series with a worker's mindset, once she had finished the series and made a billion dollars, she would have stopped writing. Is J.K. Rowling *working* on another book, or is she merely playing with one of her favorite toys: language?

Ask yourself, if you had all the money you ever needed, would you still be doing what you are doing? If you can answer *"yes"* to that, then congratulations! You are already earning passive income. You are not working at all, as you are engaged in play. If you answered *"no"* to that, or if you gave a harsher answer, then you have the power to reconsider the character you are playing. You will know you are closing in on becoming the character you were created to play *when love is effortless.*

A lion is not the fastest, largest, or the smartest animal in the jungle. The cheetah, the elephant, the hyena, and the crocodile all have their claim to the throne. Yet the lion remains king because the lion sees itself as king. You are never stuck with any idea of yourself. There exist many outdated and inaccurate versions of you in the minds of your associates, and they have no force over you. Those who are open to new information will experience your new character and conform accordingly. Those who do not will find themselves irrelevant in your new play.

This does not necessarily mean you are throwing people out of the theater. The theater has many rows of seats. The front row is reserved for your VIPs: your family, your co-creators, your best friends. You are in charge of the seating chart. If your evolved character chooses to move people to the back rows, that is not disloyalty. You are not being asked to stop loving them. You can love them from afar, while giving yourself an atmosphere and context this new character will be best understood in.

From this new vantage point, perhaps you will become a model for them to transcend a trial of their own; one you would have never overcome had you made yourself responsible for their evolution as well as your own. It is a paradox, the world is filled with them, but sometimes we do love people best by letting them go, or at least, by practicing non-attachment. Our attachments can hold both of us back from stepping into power. Attachments can hold us back from *remembering*.

I have often thought that *life is long enough to be patient, but too short to waste.*

This life is not a dress rehearsal. You are on the stage, playing it out. If an attachment to an idea about your character is preventing you from living the life you want to live, then why are you believing it? The only reason to not believe in yourself is if you are an atheist with a God complex. I am not suggesting that Rudy or someone of his stature could believe his way to being a powerhouse running back. But I am encouraging you to not let your dream walk out the door in the backpack of perceived inadequacies. Why not you? Why not take those dreams and make them real? You can. That version of yourself in ten years who is living it out exists. That version already exists in the first place that everything must exist before it can materialize: within your imagination. If you have the power to imagine your new character, then you have the power to take one step toward the alignment with him or her.

Buddha said, "Not all suffering is from attachment, but all attachment leads to suffering."

Practice non-attachment to your ideas of yourself. Die to yourself today. If you get too attached to some idea of yourself, you will hinder your evolution. Non-attachment allows you to take the vision of who you are stepping into, and welcome *any* opportunity to get into alignment. As life twists and turns in the direction of your dreams, all you have to do is stay in character.

This is not about patience. Everything you desire is already here. You do not have to hustle or grind or work to get anything. You need only step into the energy of what you desire.

Imagine you are living in a cliffside lake house with impeccable views of the sunset. You own an immense deck, and every weather-permitting morning you head out on the deck to begin your routine. You taste your morning beverage of choice, you feel the fresh air filling your lungs, you take in the gorgeous scenery, you hear the subtle sounds of people you love stirring about in the house, feel the embrace of your comfortable chair, you smell the aroma of trees and flowers and dew and something special each day carried on the wind...

Embody the energy you carry in this visualization or whichever visualization speaks most to you.

That version of you exists in the first place everything must exist: inside your mind. Spend time with that version, and eventually you will spend time *as* that version. That materialization of the cliffside house and your enjoyment of it begin now. There is not a shortcut to the house because it is already here with you now. Perhaps you cannot slide open the physical door or literally feel the wooden decking beneath your feet, but that does not make it any less real.

Jesus said, "Ask and you shall receive."

Ask Him now. What do you desire? A career that you love? Your own business? A nurturing and supportive relationship? These things are about to be presented to you. The key is not asking for them in the right way, or praying with the right words. The key is being ready to receive them when they are offered, and to be unattached to the way He wants to give them to you. The key is matching the alignment of your character with the energy of the blessing. If within your imagination, the blessing has you jumping for joy, then go ahead and jump for joy right now. You have already successfully managed the tricky part: You have visualized a future with emotional potency. Now you can jump for joy all the way into the blessing. This is the energy of play at work.

You have the power to create your future. Imagine it, embody it, carry it, and watch the physical details emerge from the ethers. This is the quantum field we spoke of earlier, with infinite possibilities, helplessly delivering to you the materials of your alignment.

become like children

Julie Cameron's *The Artist's Way* provides a ton of opportunities to strip out of the clothing that the world dresses us in, like fear, uncertainty, and doubt, and instead to adorn ourselves with the childlike spirit God gave us.

I have heard of doubt described as the first drink for an alcoholic. You cannot have but one doubtful thought in your mind. Doubt begets more doubt. The next thing you know, you are a doubt-aholic. Your imagination gets blocked, your vision becomes clouded, and thereafter you struggle to manifest any of your desires. Doubt is the playkiller.

What people who have maintained their creative connection have done is silenced doubt in its tracks. They imagine who they want to be, and they believe in their ability to be it. These transformations happen first in our imaginations long before it shows up in our reality. Napoleon Hill said, "Whatever your mind can conceive and believe, it can achieve."

Children spend their days conceiving and believing. So be like children.

Matthew 18:1-3 reads, "At that time the disciples came to Jesus, saying, 'Who is the greatest in the kingdom of heaven?' And calling to him a child, he put him in the midst of them and said, 'Truly, I say to you, unless you turn and become like children, you will never enter the kingdom of heaven.'"

This is not a threat. This is a map.

The kingdom of heaven is a place of love, connection, and creativity. The kingdom is a place where you can know God, which is akin to knowing that part of yourself He created that is just like Him. The more you know Him the more you will feel and find that same essence within yourself.

Ask any parent and they will tell you a long list of characteristics of children. Monster might make the list. They are not wrong. Children are new human beings. Most of them are not well-adjusted, clear-minded, nor highly emotionally experienced creatures. Mind the conscious differences between being childish and childlike. We have so much to learn from children at their best.

I asked my colleague, a son of a missionary, a lifelong Christ follower, and father of three boys what he thought about the aforementioned verse. I asked, "Josiah, what does it mean to you to *become like children*"?"

He told me a story about his son. He said, "When my son is playing and I am around, he does not think twice about his safety. He knows his father has him. He will bound to the top of the stairs and leap, faithfully knowing I will catch him. He does not pause. He does not doubt. He knows. His whole identity is rooted in that love and trust. He knows his father would never let anything bad happen to him."

There was a study done comparing the behavior of children on a playground with and without a fence. On the playground without, the children tended to hover closer to the teacher where they derived their sense of safety. On the playground with a fence, the children used the entire playground and were able to exhibit their freedom. When their safety was given, freedom was expressed. Otherwise, the children prioritized safety.

Josiah mentioned that his son is just learning to swim. He still cannot, though. When Josiah is in the pool, his son will jump into the deep end with little to no warning. "Dad, catch me!" he will shout and take the plunge. His son has such a deep trust in his safety around his father that there are no boundaries to his expression of freedom. He is not testing his father, he simply has unwavering trust.

"I can do all things through Christ who strengthens me," Philippians 4:13 reads. When Paul the Apostle penned these words to the congregation he had established in Philippi around 62 AD, he was in prison.

Unwavering trust. That is a childlike characteristic.

What would you do with unwavering trust? What leaps would you make?

Josiah finished the discussion with, "God is not going to let me down." For Josiah and for me, we are identified as children of the loving, attentive, protecting Father. He is there to catch us, to bandage us with His word, to pick us up, to dust us off, to always show us that our trust is not misplaced.

This trust is what allows us to exhibit our freedom. This trust washes away fear, out of sight and out of mind.

This dynamic between Abba and me is why I can play. Just like Josiah's son has his identity in the safety of his father, so mine is rooted in the safety of my Father.

"Whatever your mind can conceive and believe, it can achieve." That line would not be true for me without this Father-child dynamic. The keyword here is *whatever*. This is not limited to the small, simple things that are easy to believe in. Miracles have no degrees of magnitude in the eyes of the creator.

character building

Earlier in this chapter, I talked about finding happiness being as simple as changing the character you are playing. It is not such a simple task. Parts of our personality are composed of our conditioned thoughts and deep belief systems. We, as humans, are eternally unfinished products. Becoming who you sense is possible is a lifelong endeavor. The good news is that each day we face opportunities to *remember* ourselves. Every moment of every day we are faced with new opportunities to renew our alignment to who we are becoming.

ROMANS 12:2 READS,

"Do not conform to the pattern of this world,
but be transformed by the renewing of your mind. Then you
will be able to test and approve what God's will is—
his good, pleasing and perfect will."

Do not be *of* the world, be *in* the world. The material world wants you to think with your materials. Do not conform to the egotistical, selfish, shallow-minded patterns of the world. Be wary of advice given that allows you to close your heart. Be wary of that Justified Voice in your head that beckons you downward.

It says, "It is okay that you raged on them because they hurt you first."

It says, "They had it coming."

It says, "I will be the necessary evil" as you go fight fire with fire.

You build a lasting character from the ground up. The foundation of your new character is the character's beliefs.

If your character believes in a hostile world where everybody is out to get them, their thoughts will be aggressive and violent. Their words will be sharp and harsh. Their actions will be defensive. Their habits will be those of isolation and protection. Their character will be stuck in survival mode. According to Mazlow's hierarchy of needs, a person who spends all their time seeking their safety needs will never feel belonging and love, nor a sense of self-esteem, nor will they ever experience any of the growth that leads to their self-actualization.

It all starts with beliefs.

I believe in a loving, attentive, and present God. Belief has created a deluge of sight in my life, and I revel in the act of noticing. The synchronicities and blessings abound. Albeit, I used to think of my belief systems as BS, that my knack for optimism was merely selective seeing. I wondered if I was indulging in a delusion. The atheists in my life would point at the God of the Old Testament as evidence of this delusion. "You believe in a loving God, eh?" They would snicker. At the same time, I never doubted my parents' love for me when I was being punished. My folks never took pleasure in my punishment. They never belittled the pain of my spankings with statements like, "This hurts me more than it hurts you," but I suspect that long after my pain went away they wished for a better way to get through to me. When God was destroying Sodom or carrying out the annihilation of the Canaanites, I believe He was thinking about Jesus while sadly sighing within the words of Ezekiel: "Have I any pleasure in the death of the wicked… and not rather that He should turn from his way and live?"

LAO TZU SAID,

"Watch your thoughts, they become your words; watch your words, they become your actions; watch your actions, they become your habits; watch your habits, they become your character; watch your character, it becomes your destiny."

Your thoughts are a reflection of your beliefs. Contrary to the beliefs of many, your thoughts are your responsibility. Your body is well within your control. Sure, your heart beats and your mind thinks without your command. You are a sack of flesh, blood, and bones with an electric current running through you. Sometimes that electric current makes connections that produce odd thoughts.

The French coined a term called *l'appel du vide* - the call of the void.

Recently I was atop Angel's Landing at Zion National Park and this voice popped into my head: "Jump off", it said. Or when I am walking along the sidewalk with someone and they are on the streetside, the voice says, "Push 'em into traffic." Where this nonsense comes from I do not know, but when it happens, I have an immediate and deliberate correction. "That's just the call of the void." My good friend and open-hearted advisor Aaron likes to say, "*Silly neurons.*"

You cannot curate your mind with only happy thoughts all the time. There is an expression: *Innocence cannot project.* I am not innocent. I am human. I am made of bones, flesh, and blood and my materials are imperfect. I am an unfinished product. As my priest says about creation, "You are a good thing in a bad condition. If only you could restore your factory settings…"

Yet while my chemistry will continue to produce oddities, I can choose not to believe them. I can choose to counter them with awareness and *with* better thoughts. When I am tempted to conform to the thought patterns of the world, I can deliberately refocus my mind.

"Oops, I caught myself thinking the world was against me. I know that is not true." And then I can spend a couple minutes counting the blessings I had momentarily taken for granted.

Watch your thoughts, Lao Tzu said. He did not say *judge* your thoughts. He did not say control your thoughts. Jiddu Krishnamurti said, "The ability to observe without evaluating is the highest form of intelligence." Watch your thoughts. Be aware of your thoughts. At the end of the day, know that a random thought is just a firing of neurons. You do not have to believe your random thoughts. When you observe them without evaluating them, you are free to discern which ones are worth cultivating and which ones can be ignored. This is not a judgment. Above judgment is a recognition about what is good for you. This is a discernment of what you desire more of, and what is not serving you. If a thought is generating an egotistical rage, you can observe plainly that it will not get you what you desire. If a thought is plunging you into despair, think differently. Remember the continuous question of primary importance to the Detourist: *What Path am I on?*

"To dwell on" is a perfect way to describe our thoughts.

Our dwelling is our home.

Our minds are our dwellings, the homes we take with us.

We decorate our dwelling with our thoughts. We can choose thoughts of love or lust. Of hope or hate. Of play or pain. Of cheering or of chiding.

You have the authority to dwell on any thought you wish. A passing, random thought is a bird flying past your window. It is something to observe. If it is not going to give your world the aesthetic you desire, you do not have to invite it inside your dwelling.

MARTIN LUTHER SAID,

"You cannot prevent the birds from flying in the air over your head, but you can certainly prevent them from building a nest in your hair."

People who follow Christ often call Jesus an *indwelling*. He becomes a sort of land Lord of the mind who curates thoughts toward ideas like love, joy, peace, patience, kindness, generosity, faithfulness, gentleness, and self-control.

If you want to change your character, take ownership of your thoughts. Inspect what you believe about the world. Take the advice of Lao Tzu and *watch*. Take the wisdom of Jiddu and *observe without evaluating*.

part two

imagination

CHAPTER 2

the collide-o-scope

We have all looked through a kaleidoscope at some point. We have all gazed at the different colored crystals. In your mind's eye, imagine them spinning and fractaling out in ornate mandalas.

> *BEFORE YOU MOVE ON, YOU ARE GOING TO WANT TO DOWNLOAD YOUR FREE COPY OF THE COLLIDE-O-SCOPE. GO TO WWW.MATTHEWEMMOREY.COM/COLLIDEOSCOPE. GO AHEAD AND READ DAY 0 AND GET ACQUAINTED WITH THE ANALOGY. THE COLLIDE-O-SCOPE IS AN ANALOGY FOR YOUR AWARENESS. IT IS GOING TO BE CRITICAL FOR TRAVERSING THIS PART OF THE PATH, THE PART THAT LEADS DOWN THE ROAD OF DISCOVERY, THROUGH PLAY, INTO THE KALEIDOSCOPIC PEAKS.*

Whatever colored crystal gets embedded in the center of a kaleidoscope - *the focal point* - will divide and multiply, supplanting the colors around the center until it becomes the majority. If this focal point remains for long enough, the entire kaleidoscope will be imbued thoroughly with this color.

This is how our attention works.

Each color represents the energy behind certain thoughts and beliefs.

Someone who watches hours upon hours of Youtube conspiracy theories is continuously infusing their reality with suspicion and skepticism. On one hand, they can rest more assured that nobody can pull the wool over their eyes. Sometimes, they will be right in assigning conspiratorial motivations to the situation before them. They will avoid being hurt, tricked, scammed, defrauded, and taken advantage of...Which sounds pretty attractive.

Sometimes (*I dare say* more often), they will be wrong, and their suspicions will block blessings. They will have conditioned their field of vision with conspiracy-colored-crystals. Their mind is at-the-ready to suggest conspiracy in any situation where the truth is not readily apparent. If allowed to go unchecked, they will lose touch with reality, sinking into a bog of paranoia. This will be clear to everyone except them, as one can only be aware of the ideas with which they retain a corresponding crystal.

Hell on earth is a reality completely separate from God. It is one characterized by greed, despair, bitterness, anger, hate, and the like. If God is a pure white-light colored crystal, Hell exists in the mind that does not see or know Love anywhere. When the last pure white-light fragment is gone from their minds, a person is in Hell.

Someone does not change their *Collide-o-scope* overnight. It takes time for new colors to embed and fractal outward. It takes discipline and awareness to recognize when we are allowing a distasteful center to corrupt us. Sometimes we have to taste the bile in our mouths before we realize that we have replaced God. Sometimes it takes deep breaths, or kicking and screaming, or time in the gym hitting a bag as hard as we can in order to shake loose the black, empty seeds that want to take root in our focal points. We cannot let them. If we do, we lose.

two truths

Some friends and I took a trip to Zion National Park in Utah. We decided to hike Angel's Landing on the last day of the trip. Angel's Landing is known for being a short but strenuous hike followed by a tactical one-foot-in-front-of-the-other march to the top of a narrow 1500' tall precipice. At the top, you are treated to spectacular views of the valley and the river that carved it out. These days, the last 3/4 mile is a logjam of hikers of vastly different ages and skill levels. The popularity of the hike entices a lot of people who quickly become out of their depth.

My friend Vic coaxed our group and others on with the mantra: *Hand on the chain, eyes on your footing.*

The trail has gotten so popular and crowded on weekends that the stop and go traffic creates ample opportunities to people-watch. In the past few years, numerous people have misstepped and fallen to their deaths on the hike, and the fact of this reality is plastered across many faces. Some people are frozen with fear, their eyes wet with tears, sitting immovably on the side of the trail.

"Don't look down," one hiker says to another as they traverse the narrowest part of the pass. The ground falls away a few steps to either side. A thousand feet down, jagged rocks await the climber who takes a miscalculated step.

"Believe me, I'm not going to," she responds.

"Did you see that sign back there?"

"No, what did it say?" she asks.

"It noted how many people have fallen to their deaths here."

"Okay, that's enough talking please," she breathes with exasperation.

Hands on the chain, eyes on your footing. Focus on your security and your objective. Do not focus on the catastrophic possibilities lurking in wait. Try to avoid getting your heart in your throat. Keep your mind on the task at hand. *Focus.*

One by one we maneuvered to the top and then back down again. Michael, the friend in my group who had been candid about his crippling fear of heights, was not crippled. He kept his head. He did not let his fear take him out of the chase.

Did you know the subconscious mind processes 27,500 times more data than the conscious mind? The brain takes in 11,000,000 bits of data per second, but the conscious mind can only process around 400 of those bits.

quick exercise in mindfulness

Focus on your big toe.

Now your other big toe.

Now focus on your pinkies.

Listen to all the sounds one by one that you
can pick out of the airwaves.

Try to find sensations in your body / your awareness that you were
not aware of a moment ago. They were there a moment ago, but
you were not conscious of them.

Your subconscious is like a giant database, and your consciousness is like a search engine. All of this information is available to you whenever you want to concentrate on it. The moment you concentrate on something, you become part of it. Your conscious mind immerses itself into the subject, and while all of the other possibilities remain, they disappear into the annals of the database. Until you are ready to focus on something else.

For the first hiker, the one that framed the views as dangerous and mentioned the sign warning death, I would wager he had filled his conscious mind with all the treacherous possibilities. In the search engine, he typed "*what could go wrong?*" I do not think he was taunting or tormenting his female companion. Perhaps it was a coping mechanism for him. The words whistling out of his mouth were like the steam from a tea kettle letting off pressure. The pressure that had accumulated in his mind was due to the environs he had created there. You cannot focus on the negative possibilities of a situation for very long before the tension begins to build. You cannot hold that tension easily, so you accidentally or deliberately share the burden.

Frank Herbert wrote in *Dune*, "I must not fear. Fear is the mind-killer. Fear is the little-death that brings total obliteration."

Therein lies the power of Vic's mantra: *Hands on the chain, eyes on your footing.* We, as human beings, do not have unlimited focus. In fact, as I mentioned above, we have extremely limited focus. Our eyes do most of the heavy lifting for our subconscious, processing about 90% of the 11,000,000 bits per second. On Angel's Landing and in life, "*out of sight, out of mind*" is a potent reality.

If your hands are on the chain and your eyes are on your footing, your consciousness cannot be anywhere else. Robin Sharma said, "Your mind is a wonderful servant, but a terrible master." If you are in command of your focus, your mind will go where you direct it. If you dismiss ownership of your brain to itself, it will hit you with emotional electricity like lightning strikes.

Bill Murray said, "You are better at everything when you are relaxed."

cookieception

In sight, in mind is also true.

I had a hankering for cookies one afternoon. So I organized the butter next to the chocolate chips in the fridge. I made a comment to Bella about organizing the baking cabinet, and that she should check out my handiwork.

A couple hours later, she exclaimed, "I think I am going to bake cookies!"

the collide-o-scope

I was sitting at a table in Tulum, Mexico in the summer of 2021 for a yoga teacher training. The table was a work of art, constructed of meticulously interconnected pieces of wood which created a mandala of the table top.

I sat at that table with a friend who was also attending the yoga teacher training. We drank fresh juice and coffee and munched on a brick oven pizza. I stared down with appreciation at the delicious morsels of nourishment, and haphazardly listened to my friend complain about things.

"It makes me soooo sad, Matt," she said. "The pollution in the ocean has created so much sargasso weed that it ruined the beach. It's disgusting. The fish are dying. The water is unswimmable. It smells bad. It's gross. It's just terrible."

"What can we do about it?" I finally asked her. I was hoping that taking action would cheer her up.

"I don't know," she said. "It's so sad. I was here a couple months ago and the beaches were pristine. Now they are ruined."

I looked back down at the mandala table. Strewn about the table, divided up into little sections of the mandala was the pizza, my juice, my coffee, my water, my napkin, a few sachets of sweetener, and a little cup and saucer of oat milk. In that moment, I could see how each section of the mandala was like a little *focus*; somewhere different I could plant my attention. I could think about my napkin and all the waste in the world, and I could really dwell on it painfully as my friend was. On the other side of the spectrum, there was a cheesy pizza with a bubbled crust and various delectable toppings. I could dwell on that with a few of my senses, and get lost just as easily in its deliciousness.

Both truths exist simultaneously. There is the existence of the sargassum weed and the very distracting, delicious pizza. There is a kaleidoscope of ever-shifting potential focuses. You can only focus on one at a time. Focusing on one does not render the others non-existent. Together they all comprise reality. However, your mind is changed into a container for whatever you focus on. You can subject it to focuses that depress you, or you can subject it to focuses that enliven and enrich you. Or you can use it to find solutions to the ugliness inspired by goodness - I call these *Loving Solutions*.

The presence of the weed is due in part to warmer, nutrient dense waters - nutrients that have come from increased runoff of agricultural inputs and sewage from the Amazon. It is also due to changing ocean currents, a lack of hurricanes recently, and climate change.

I did not want to think about seaweed while I was eating my pizza, and I eventually changed the subject. I can appreciate how much my friend cares about environmental issues. I love to see people engaged in the dangerous act of caring about something. I care about the environment, too, but I tend to look at things differently than the person who fixates on the problems. I have an immutable optimism about the world and its direction so issues like this do not affect my mood so much. Some might call that optimism reckless. Or feckless. I disagree. I believe that humans will get it right before it's too late. I believe that people are inherently good. It is a matter of focus. It is easy to look out at all the issues people have created and be nihilistic. It is easy to believe that humans are inherently bad.

The evidence of our failings as a species abound. We can focus on those failings and call it reality. Many people do. They walk around with sour ideas about the world, because they have selected a narrow, pessimistic focus. Their pessimism is reinforced by projecting negativity onto circumstances. They can hardly help it, as the state of their mind, or the color of their *Collide-o-scopes*, powerfully dictates how they interpret new information.

The evidence of our beauty as a species abounds, just the same. To focus on this would not allow you to see more of the truth, but another truth. To call the best in people and the best in the world true reality is its own form of naivety.

People want the world to be black and white so they can understand it. It's not. It's an ever-shifting, bright, and colorful kaleidoscope. There is darkness, light, and everything in between. What is important to know is that whatever you focus on envelops your mind. Whatever you focus on you become. This is what you create more of.

Remember, "God saw all that he had made, and it was very good." This does not mean that humans do not occasionally get it wrong. We get it wrong all the time. We are a good thing in a bad condition. There is only one way to restore our factory settings. There is one universal solution.

In my own life, I have been tempted to believe that I have thousands of different problems. In this delusion each of these problems has its own solution, so I have constant work cut out for me. I have a field of vision with many discolored crystals, indeed. However, anytime I re-center with Love and not self, everytime I make something sacred with my sacrifice, or in short, whenever I am in grace my problems disappear. My problems wax and wane in correlation with my connection with Love. Logically, I must not have a thousand problems. I must have only one: *Disconnection*. God has been dislodged from the center of my *Collide-o-scope*.

Am I saying that I will never do anything about the sargassum problem or environmental issues because it's *in God's hands*? Not at all. I try not to use my spirituality to bypass real issues in my life. I won't look away from issues because I do not want them to be true...But it is possible to simultaneously be aware of the issue without becoming part of it. Despair always adds to the problem.

I desire to be face to face with my Creator, to allow myself to be led by God. To trust in Him in all things, including environmental issues like this, and to say, "Call on me and I will go." I am always listening for my name. This dynamic allows me to be led by my Father, not my emotions. My unwavering optimism exists because I believe that God is inevitable. I believe that people are good. As Walt Whitman wrote in the opening poem, in all things, there is the seed perfection. I believe that the solution will come about in an unforeseeable way through our connection to God and each other. *I really, truly trust.*

loving solutions

Apenimon loved his new role. It allowed him to drive around, spend time outdoors, speak with clients, and problem solve. Under his influence, sales had climbed month over month. Client satisfaction was on the rise. Projects under his supervision tended to be larger and more inspired. Per the suggestion of one customer, the marketing materials for the lumberyard were being redone with samples of their latest projects. Each of the featured photographs were from projects championed by Apenimon.

The success at work allowed Apenimon to improve his living situation. He moved out of his studio apartment and into a house, he bought a brand new Chevy, and began saving for his future. Strangely, upon opening a savings account at the credit union, he realized an image had appeared out of the fog of his imagination: *a future*. Up until this point, thinking of *what might be* was a risk he had never dared. But now he was selling some of his old belongings and making room for the new. He was not clinging to security, but taking some chances on himself.

However, not everything was going perfectly.

Apenimon was finding it difficult to hire good laborers. A few, with quiet prejudices, had quit upon his promotion. A few others had left as the workload increased. The remaining core was exceptional, but there were only so many of them, with only so much energy. To top it off, his best employee, Martin, was going through an odd season. Martin was getting about half of his normal work done, and as he slacked off, the rest of the crew followed his leadership. It seemed Apenimon's windfall of success was coming to an end...

So Apenimon was a bit stressed.

The next day at work, as he was pulling into the lumberyard, a boy on a bright orange bike nearly crashed into the side of his new truck. "No brakes!" the boy shouted as he whizzed by. *Bad start to the day.*

Seeing Martin that day at the job site triggered Apenimon. The laborer was standing still, his hammer held limp at his side, staring off into space. *We don't have time for this*, Apenimon thought. Scolding words welled up in his mouth and he prepared to spit them at Martin.

As he approached, something else overcame him. He saw anguish in Martin's body language. The man's face was pulled in a grimace, as though something was causing him great pain. When Martin saw the boss coming, he snapped out of his daze. "Getting back at it. Sorry, boss."

"Hold on a sec, Marty," Apenimon said. Instead of scolding him, the boss asked Martin what was going on in his life. He could tell something was up, and despite Martin's attempts to hide it, he could tell. In that conversation, Martin revealed that his mother was dying of cancer. He occasionally paused throughout the day to pray for her. Martin told him he did not mean to slack off, but he was just so easily distracted lately.

The conversation ended when Apenimon had an idea. He patted Martin on the back and went to discuss something with the foreman and the crew. With the foreman's approval and the crew's buy-in, Apenimon approached Martin at lunch with an idea.

"We are giving you Wednesday afternoons off for the foreseeable future.

You will still be paid. The crew has agreed to cover for you, so you can go sit at your mom's bedside."

"No," Martin argued. "That's not fair."

"Well, life's not fair, Marty," Apenimon said, patting the man on the back again. "Starting today. Starting now. We will manage without you." Although Apenimon sounded confident, he was much less sure on the inside. The crew would have to work hard to replace Marty, and although they did seem willing to help, the honest man was wary.

Over the next couple months, something miraculous happened. When Marty was at work, he was setting the tone. He *worked*. He was eager to repay the crew's kindness tenfold, and he routinely went out of his way to alleviate their workload. He raved about the extra time with his mom. They were getting along well, and he was able to make a big difference with her. But finally, the fateful day came when Martin arrived at work hanging his head. His mother had passed. When he saw Apenimon that day, he gave him a tremendous hug. Martin told him that the extra time with his mom was precious, maybe the most special memories he had with her. He was eternally grateful.

To Apenimon's surprise, Martin began carrying a banner for the lumberyard. Everywhere the man went, he overwhelmed the public with cheers for the incredible employer that allowed him to spend his mother's final days at her bedside.

It was not long before applications began stacking up on Apenimon's desk. Many of them cited hearing Martin's story. They were eager to work with such an honest, caring, generous man such as Apenimon. Suddenly, unexpectedly, hiring hardworking crews was no trouble at all.

There was a warm fire burning in Apenimon's heart when he left the lumberyard that day. But then he saw it. The side of his new truck was scratched from the driver's door to the back wheel well, streaked in bright orange paint. Immediately, Apenimon knew the culprit. That dang kid with the bike with no brakes! He should have seen this coming.

To Apenimon's delight, he knew exactly where that reckless boy lived.

He made a quick stop before going to the boy's house. When he got there, he knocked loudly on the front door. After a couple knocks, a woman came hesitantly to the door. "Is that your son's bike?" Apenimon asked at once. The man could not help but notice the bike had been damaged, no doubt when it had collided with his new truck.

"What did he do now?" the woman groaned.

"Can you get him for me?"

The woman called for her son. A minute later, he appeared in the doorway. When he saw Apenimon's truck, his face flushed. He tried to turn and run, but his mother held him in place.

"We have a problem," Apenimon began gruffly. "The same problem, I think. I have a new truck that I don't want scratched and you have a route you take on a bike with no brakes. It was just a matter of time before this happened."

"I…I…" the boy stammered.

"Say you're sorry!" his mother demanded.

"I'm sorry!" the boy said.

"I accept your apology," Apenimon said. He then backed up and went to the tailgate of his truck. He clicked the gate open and retrieved something. "But sorry is not going to prevent my truck from being scratched again, is it?" Apenimon then pulled a new mountain bike from the truck's bed and presented it to the boy. "But this might."

✦　✦　✦

"Nothing transforms in a field of judgment."

– AMANDA GOOLSBY

For every problem, there is a loving solution. There are a lot of "activists" out there exacerbating the problem in their attempt to solve it. If the one problem we have is a separation from Love, then any issue that we address from separation only mutates our problem. We go from knowing the issue to being the issue.

> ## "We cannot solve our problems with the same thinking we used when we created them."
>
> - ALBERT EINSTEIN

In Columbia, coffee is one of the prime crops. There are animals that live in the hills where the coffee grows, and it becomes problematic for the farmers to have their crops eaten by these animals. This is their livelihood.

The farmer could load up a shotgun and head out onto the land. He could start picking these petulant critters off one by one. The farmer, in a field of judgment, is not far from citing ownership of the land. Along with ownership comes the right to make the rules, to deem purpose, and to handle obstructions to that purpose accordingly. Farmers, after all, have dominion over the creatures on his or her land, do they not?

In Texas, coyotes are strung up on the fences around ranches. Coyotes kill lambs, calves, and other livestock, so the canines get marked as destructive pests. They are shot and hung out for other coyotes as a warning. This is commonplace. We have the guns and we have the bullets, and for as long as there has been man there have been beasts to be at odds with. However, coyotes are opportunists. They eat cactus fruit, mesquite beans, flowers, insects, rodents, lizards, rabbits, birds, and snakes. They have a lot they can survive on - it does not have to be livestock.

The squirrels of Columbia and the coyotes in Texas have as much a right to the resources of the land as the landowners. While these animals can be deemed petulant under the right conditions from the right perspective, they are just trying to solve their own problems.

The loving solution takes everyone into consideration. It does not judge, blame, punish, or retaliate.

In Columbia, the conditions are great for growing fruit and avocado trees. The destructive pests that enjoy coffee beans can also sustain themselves on fruit. So, the coffee farmers plant fruit trees in their fields intermixed with the coffee. The fruit trees can provide some shade for the coffee, and it succeeds in deterring the pests from getting at their livelihood. Naturally, they will also have some avocados leftover. The animals get to continue living symbiotically with the farmers, and the farmers do not have to address the new problems that would be created by the "pests" absence.

This is what activism looks like. It employs loving solutions.

If the ranchers looked at their problem with hungry coyotes, not as the existence of coyotes but the hunger of the coyotes, they might come up with alternate solutions. Coyotes are a keystone species. They play a vital ecological role. They reduce the number of nest predators which helps maintain healthy ecosystems and species diversity. Ironically, according to Project Coyote, killing them also destabilizes their packs. This leads them to seek out mates sooner which magnifies the population rather than diminishes it. The "problem" addressed without Love is not only temporarily mutated, but eventually worsened.

Lao Tzu said, ""It is only when a mosquito lands on your testicles that you realize there is always a way to solve problems without violence."

Without Love, you are making mayhem. With Love, you are making more problems. Just because you and the "pests" have different interests, it does not mean there is not a mutually beneficial solution. We ought to strive for solutions where more love is created and shared.

Loving solutions create an environment where everything changes for the better. The butterfly effect of a loving solution is often unforeseeable. An employer who sacrifices for the betterment of an employee creates a raving fan. The dangerous bicyclist receiving a functional bicycle protects future dents and dings, and opens an attractor field of similarly loving potential.

We want to be loved, but not second. We want love to warrant our effort. We want the things that we are loving to deserve the love, to *earn* the love, to always be worthwhile. However this will never work. An unloving action when a loving solution is possible opens a different sort of attractor field. The killing of coyotes, for example, multiplies the coyote population, literally magnifying the problem. Hate begets hate. Violence begets violence.

"You have heard that it was said, 'An eye for an eye and a tooth for a tooth.' 39But I say to you, Do not resist the one who is evil. But **if anyone slaps you on the right cheek, turn to him the other also.**"

As stated above, coyotes are opportunistic scavengers. While offering them alternatives might work, grand pyrenees make great ranch dogs. Donkeys will also keep coyotes away. The adoption of a new ranch animal will provide love, labor, and companionship.

The loving solution always bears fruit. Sometimes literally.

The unloving effort is an attempt to overwhelm the forces of nature. At no point will solving issues without love make us victorious. Mother Nature will not be cowed into submission. No matter how powerful our egos tell us we are, none of us come close to being God. To address a problem without love is to misunderstand the problem in the first place. Prepare for a lifelong game of *whack-a-mole*.

The same thinking could be applied in the Amazon, where agricultural runoff is dumping nutrients like nitrogen into the oceans and fueling massive sargassum and algae blooms. The same thinking could be applied everywhere.

My vegan friend, without knowing it, was distraught over the effects of over-agriculture. Veganism has its carbon footprint, as well. Clear-cutting massive strips of land for farming eliminates the self-sustaining vegetation of the land, progressively removes all the nutrients, and displaces or kills tons of animals. Farming is sold to us as a sustainable practice, but Earth is finite. Eventually, should our population continue to grow, should we continue to make more farms, we will run out of Earth. Native populations of old, who lived in balance with their region, were less hunter-gatherers and were more trapper-gardeners. They shared the environment rather than separated themselves from it. They were not competing with Mother Nature, they were engaged in a dance with her. They planted what they needed beneath forest canopies, paid attention to their population and its effect on their food sources, and they understood the psychic price of taking life. If you killed an animal, you also processed it. You felt the psychic weight of taking life. In essence, you paid the true price. In paying the true price, you realize the necessity of using every bit of that creation. If we all paid the psychic price of our dietary habits, it is likely that we would end up building gardens and finding more scrumptious ways to cook plants. For the animals we raise, knowing that slaughter is inevitable, we might compensate them for their sacrifice with magnificent lives.

As Ford Motor Company was growing, they found themselves with mounds of leftover carbon. Instead of seeing it as waste, they repurposed that carbon and began selling it. That adjacent company became known as Kingsford Charcoal.

Whether you are my vegan friend distraught over the seaweed bloom, an environmental activist, a rancher, a farmer, somebody who takes the garbage out a couple times a week, or merely someone with a problem, look for the opportunities to approach your problem differently. The problem was not created by God, and it will certainly not be fixed in His absence.

If sustainability interests you, I recommend a book called *Unlearn, Rewild: Earth Skills, Ideas and Inspiration for the Future Primitive* by Miles Olson.

making vs. co-creating

There is a big difference between what you *make* and what you *co-create*.

Love is another word for Creation. Creation is another word for Love. What is created with love is everlasting. When two people put their Love together, they create life. They are using creation energy to bring something eternal into the world. Its physical parts may pass away, but Love is the fabric of the spirit. The spirit is immortal.

If it is made without love, it is not created. Only love creates. Everything we make eventually expresses its impermanence. If it is made without love, it is merely an illusion. It is a puff of smoke and a trick of perception. One can point at an illusion and be truthful about seeing it, but that does not make it real.

What God has created in love cannot be undone whereas what it made without love must be continuously maintained. That is why God is inevitable. God *is* Love. When God creates, he does so in the only way he can - lovingly, eternally. You did not make yourself. *You* were created.

The ego is a jealous maker. The ego is the epitome of temporary. It tells you that you are it and it is you. It assures you that your life is the span in which you draw breath in this body. That is true for ego, but that is not true for You. The ego deals in illusions. It must continually maintain. It must draw your attention with sleight of hand, like a cunning magician. It will do so with the invention of stories, drama, danger, fear, and separation. Wayne Dyer says ego stands for edging God out. If we edge God out, we wake up with the world on our shoulders. If it's all on us, we are weighed down by pressure.

There is no wonder the ego feels threatened. It has made a world where you are disconnected, endangered, and carrying the weight of the world. Fortunately, this world will crumble away if you let it. It is as temporary as the ego, and only what is temporary can be threatened. There is no threat to what is permanent.

Your ego might be in danger, but your real Self is invulnerable.

IF YOU WANT LOVING SOLUTIONS TO COME MORE EASILY, GO TO WWW.MATTHEWEMMOREY.COM/COLLIDEOSCOPE AND DOWNLOAD A COPY OF THE COLLIDE-O-SCOPE.

divinity and duality

Walt Whitman, in the poem, *Song of the Universal*, wrote:

"COME said the Muse,
Sing me a song no poet yet has chanted,
Sing me the universal.

In this broad earth of ours,
Amid the measureless grossness and the slag,
Enclosed and safe within its central heart,
Nestles the seed perfection.

By every life a share or more or less,
None born but it is born, conceal'd or unconceal'd
the seed is waiting."

Most of us have a voice inside our heads. As we walk down the street, it narrates. "There's a tree. There's a squirrel. There's water rushing down that river from the recent rain storm. Oh, there's a trail over there!"

Chances are, your inner voice is talking now. It is probably commenting on one thing or another, drawing your attention from here to there, from this to that.

Are you this voice?

Or are you merely witnessing it?

I argue that your ability to listen to it proves that you are something else. *It* is not *you*. You are the observer. The inner voice is like the narrator of your conscious mind. It's the firing of neurons through your fleshy brain triggered by visual stimuli. It is your materials trying to make sense of the world's materials. *It is an unreliable narrator.*

Michael Singer, in *Untethered Soul*, refers to your inner voice as the roommate who never shuts up.

This inner voice is inside you, but it is not you. You are the observer of it. There is no need to identify with this voice or the ideas it has. It is not you. You do not have to believe everything that this voice thinks. Your heart beats, and your brain thinks. This brain is designed to be your servant, not your master, as Robin Sharma pointed out.

Therefore, we must differentiate your two parts. There is the observer and the voice. There is your created Self and your ego. There is your Nature and your nature. There is your humanness and your seed perfection. Henceforth, we will distinguish these two parts as Divinity and your duality.

Divinity is your spiritual birthright. Your duality is your material condition, your indivi*duality*.

Your Divinity is God within you. It is your highest intuition. It is the Truth that answers out of the quieted mind. It remains eternally and continuously connected to Source. There is nothing that jars it loose from its loving knowing. It does not *perceive* as a trick of the mind, where events are observed and evaluated. Instead, Divinity *knows*. Divinity sees with the eyes of

God and loves with His open heart. It is a champion of cooperation, a noticer of synchronicity, the experiencer of beauty. Divinity is actively loving your life, is embracing challenges, is suggesting loving solutions, and is leading with an unprojecting innocence. It is the Love that never turns its back on you or anyone else. It is a savior by the name Christ. It is perfect and unchanging and unchangingly perfect. It is not *yours*. You and everyone else share in it. It is your anchor in God. It is His intention for you.

Your duality is indivi*duality*. It is of your own making. It is a machine of perception, designing good and bad, right and wrong, black and white. Duality, means a contrast between two aspects of something. It is the champion of preference, and because it prefers, it also rejects. For everything it deems good there is an equal and opposite. Your duality is an exhausted judge. It knows not what it needs, yet it pretends to. It decides what is acceptable and what is not. It lives with one foot in reality and the other in a dream, because it has all its own ideas of how life ought to be. Duality deals in shoulds, denials, and expectations, and it uses these fickle tools in an attempt to remake the world. Duality keeps its heart open when it gets its way, but it is always ready to snap it shut. It likes and dislikes, it allows and rejects, it approves and disapproves, it evaluates and rates, yet it always struggles on its own to know what is meant for it.

If you burn your mouth on hot coffee, Divinity rejoices at the opportunity to experience humanness and all its accompanying sensations. Your duality judges wrongness.

If you are stuck in traffic behind a particular slow car, Divinity knows that you are being protected and that you will arrive exactly the moment you are meant to. *Better to recognize even that nice thought is a guess.* Better to merely say, Divinity knows. Your duality thinks, "This other person must be a complete idiot to not exist in accordance with my convenience."

If you are going through a break-up, Divinity acknowledges you have gained an opportunity for realignment. Divinity knows that nothing that is meant for you will ever pass you by. How could it? Divinity also knows that you will never keep what is not meant for you. Your duality mourns what you have lost without considering what you have gained. It is sad, devastated, angry, even closed-hearted because it had concocted conditions around your love. Meanwhile, Divinity's love is *unconditional*. Because of this, Divinity enjoys unconditionality - a sensation of complete trust and invulnerability, where nothing could happen that would get one to become closed-hearted.

If you did not get hired for a job you desperately wanted, Divinity celebrates the good sense of the employers sparing you from a path less than your highest good. It knows that something better is around the corner. It already knows that everything is worked out, and it dances forward trusting, peaceful, content, relaxed, joyous, timeless, certain, faithful, present, and jubilant instead of waiting. Your duality waits, either patiently or impatiently, but waits nonetheless. Something is missing and it is waiting, wanting. It may even be filling its head with steam, getting angry, frustrated about being overlooked, resenting those who are not forthcoming with ill-matched chances to prove itself to them. Your duality needs to prove itself. It's worth is rooted in a comparison to others. While Divinity cooperates with the world, your Duality competes. There are winners and losers to duality. To it, life is a zero-sum game. There is a finite number of spaces in the puzzle, and countless extra pieces. Your duality sees winners and losers, while Divinity sees blessings and opportunities to share.

If you look around the world and see pain, war, hunger, and suffering, Divinity does not lose faith. Your duality questions God. Your duality asks questions like, "If God is real, how could He allow such things?" Divinity holds an anchor in love for these suffering people. This anchor champions a higher ideal. It beckons you upward. It beckons you not to pass blame to God, but to re-*member*. It hangs onto the awareness of this injustice for you, so you may feel urged to "Be the change you wish to see in the world." Your duality fights back. It says, "I am something separate" while Divinity says, "We are all one body." Divinity suggests solutions, and they are loving because Divinity is the essence of Love itself. Your duality says, "Somebody needs to be punished!"

but Divinity repeats, *"We are all one body."* The imaginer of punishment is always the first to receive the punishment.

Divinity holds Love up like a billboard. Love is always in your awareness. When your individuality and God are in alignment, you experience bliss. Your heart is wide open, you love your neighbor as yourself, you have no enemies, you welcome life in its entirety, and your eyes see naught but light and opportunities to shine yours. You glow! Your *Collide-o-scope* is rich with pure white-light. You see God everywhere you look.

the gift of contrast

However, Divinity and your duality do not always agree. Yet the fact remains, Divinity is always grounded in love. This constant will occasionally provide for you a contrast. If your duality begins to express its preferences, if it begins to reject, to judge, to condemn, to perceive in ways that close your heart, you will sense the disagreement within you. If Divinity is light, contrast is the shadow cast by your duality as it impedes the light. The notions of your individuality will produce varied emotions like disgust, anger, fear, hatred, and despair. Then your duality will introduce the judge, who makes pronouncements, who bangs the gavel, who cleverly justifies being maligned. Your duality will try to convince you that you are right. Again it says, "Somebody needs to be punished. They won't learn if they are not punished. This is what they get. They deserve it! They hurt me first!" And then, if you are listening, you will remember that Divinity is invulnerable. The only part of you that could be hurt is the parts you have invented. It is not your inner Self who is hurt, it is your ego. Your ego, your inner voice, your materials, your invention, your illusion, your precious indivi*duality*. You are not hurt. You have become misaligned.

Divinity stays grounded in what is good, true, and beautiful. Divinity is God's knowledge. If you are experiencing an opposition to reality, that contrast arises between your individual perspective and God. Opposition such as this creates pain. Use contrast as a barometer of your alignment. The part of you from which love abounds knows you as invulnerable.

Contrast can be your indicator that you have closed your heart. There is only one way to return to Love. There is only one way to restore your factory settings, to return to your wholly loving condition. Put this in God's hands. Re-open your heart. Swallow the hard knot. Take a deep breath. Forget yourself. Turn back to love before you are lost.

phantom pain

Erwin McManus compares the contrast between Divinity and duality to phantom pain.

Phantom pain is the post-amputation phenomenon where a person feels pain coming from a body part that's no longer there. There once was a connection and now there is not. A person only experiences phantom pain of what they once had.

In the garden of Eden, whether this is a spiritual place or a historical one, we were one with God. For a moment, we did not have an overactive, perceptive mind. We had a knowledge of what was meant for us, and so we could go through life without judgment. We were innocent, and all we could project onto the world was innocence. We loved the earth and all creation. Love grounded us in Divinity. It was perfect armor within which we were invulnerable. Because, of course, we did not think of ourselves. We dwelled in the world as a whole. We lived this high ideal. We expressed Divinity, and it was very good.

And then we began choosing ourselves. We fell from Divinity into duality. We ate the fruit of the tree of the knowledge of good and evil. The judge was born. An awareness of duality was born. We took up this new tool and we used it. We overused it. We became like the caricature in the expression, "To a hammer, every problem looks like a nail" or rather, the person who finds a gavel begins to think they are a judge. Our judge, with gavel in hand, began to edge God out. We began to develop a sense of self-importance. We began to think we had it all figured out. We began to listen to ourselves instead of our highest intuition. Our decisions were maligned by justifications, and by and by, we made ourselves out to be mini gods. Later, when our malalignment became malignant, we did not take personal responsibility. We found a way to blame God for our choices. "How could a loving God allow such suffering?" we asked. The answer was drowned out by our own banging gavel.

Between the thumping, there was another voice. A quiet one. A loving one. A constant one ready to be listened to. A higher ideal. It had been millenia, yet there still existed an awareness of what we had abandoned. Our nature has not changed. Divinity still holds up a billboard for Love, and so we retain an awareness, a phantom pain, a nudge of contrast, of a forgone connection.

Anytime there is a disparity between our duality and Divinity, between ourselves and God, we will experience pain. This pain is informative. It wants you to feel into it, to understand it, to observe it without evaluating it, and to respond accordingly. Pain is part of the human experience. You will not evolve beyond it. It ought not be shamed away, blocked, told stories about, or identified with. It is merely information. Contrary to popular interpretation, our pain is actually a gift. It is an alarm system. It is a moment by moment instruction manual on maintaining an open heart. You can read it, or you can pretend it does not exist.

Buddha said, "Not all suffering is from attachment, but all attachment leads to suffering."

Suffering may be the result of love. Jesus suffered for our sins. But often, suffering is an indication of contrast. We suffer because we have closed our hearts, because we are *unsurrendered*. We are unaccepting of reality because we deem reality unacceptable. We end up living with one foot in truth and the other in delusion, because the delusion makes life palatable. But living out of touch with reality, attached to our delusions, does not solve anything. Our problems persist, manifesting in a thousand different ways. More *Whack-a-mole*.

Carl Jung said, "What you resist not only persists, but will grow in size."

Reinhold Neibuhr wrote the Serenity prayer. It goes:

"God, give me grace to accept with serenity
the things that cannot be changed,
Courage to change the things
which should be changed,
and the Wisdom to distinguish
the one from the other.
Living one day at a time,
Enjoying one moment at a time,
Accepting hardship as a pathway to peace,
Taking, as Jesus did,
This sinful world as it is,
Not as I would have it,
Trusting that You will make all things right,
If I surrender to Your will,
So that I may be reasonably happy in this life,
And supremely happy with You forever in the next.
Amen."

If life comes down to reality or preference, reality will win 100% of the time.

Good news: This moment provides us everything that we need regardless of how we treat it.

Divine guidance takes a keen ear to hear already. It will certainly be missed if it is drowned out by noisy gaveling.

who am i?

In December 2017, I sat on my couch with my head in my hands. Scattered around me were the remnants of broken old things. I hid their reminders of my shame beneath new things. These new things excited me! Distracted me! Beginnings always did. There was an anonymous playfulness to new beginnings, where much is allowed to remain mysterious. The closeness *feels* intimate, but it is yet a calculation. I wrap myself up in mystery like swaddling clothes. How comfortable I am, how free I am, how exciting this is, this new beginning...

I had cast the old things with which I shared history aside. I must make room for the new and exciting! And yet, a moment after dancing gleefully in anticipation of my new life, I cupped my head in my hands and cried, "*Nobody knows me.*"

I was not yet ready to look at myself as the architect of my depression. The notion of ownership was far too overwhelming. I had peeked my head inside the rabbit hole before, and nearly drowned in an upwelling of guilt and shame. *People like this version of me*, I thought, *the one I show them*. I figured it was easier to remain liked and anonymous.

But it isn't.

A liked, anonymous thing has no form. It has no boundaries. It has no substance. It has no character. It is an amorphous, shapeless, imaginary unknown. This is an unhappy creature. Deep down, it mopes about the unimportance of its existence.

This unhappy creature will continue to be unhappy until it learns to be vulnerable. Vulnerability is a massive act of courage. Also, logically, the amorphous blob has nothing to lose by taking a shape. One like this chooses between slow decline into obscurity, carrying misery all the way, or of vulnerability, the potential to be discarded. At worst, this creature risks making an effort without effect. Why does the fear of failure drive a person to never try? Why do we think we can live with our never-trying selves more easily than the version who tries and fails? Why do we assume that trying will teach us nothing, and that we deserve to be miserable? If only this were true...

But it isn't.

The guarded, anonymous, unhappy, shapeless thing is already struggling to live with itself. Vulnerability becomes a desperate attempt at living. The creature has no other option, unless withering away without living is palatable.

But it isn't.

My hands are cupped around my crying face. I asked myself a desperate question: *Who am I?*

The creature fiddles with a flipbook of memories. In each one, it leaves behind a trail of brokenness, tears, pain, and suffering. The creature has heard of the Midas' touch, where everything the king touched turned to gold. The creature presumes it has something of the opposite. "Everything I touch turns to shit," it thinks.

The flipbook reveals scenes of the creature's depravity. The creature thinks, "I am a liar, a cheat, a thief, and a burden. I break everything that I touch. I am The Boy who Breaks Things."

The evidence of my identity abounded. The more I looked, the more I found reminders of my brokenness. Brokenness reflected back at me from everywhere I looked, and of course, I looked only for brokenness.

The creature began to take shape. "I am The Boy who Breaks Things," it thought. "It fits. Though I do not wish to break them."

identity

"Who am I?"
The voice inside my head would like to know.
I ask on his behalf.
The one who hears him inside my head would also like to know:
"Who am I?"
No, before you answer either, we agree, the question is actually,
"Who are we?"

Our identities are so important to us. The question "who am I?" has reverberated through the minds of humans since the beginning. We want to know so badly that we search in unlikely places. Our hearts hunger for the answer. Occasionally, we substitute our preferences, our relationships, our hobbies, and our history for the answer. We treat the sentence "I am..." as though it is incomplete.

"Who are you?" they ask.

"I am."

And then people wait for you to finish. As much as they want to define themselves, they want to define you. They scour the physical world for spiritual answers. Penelope Douglas said, "We all eat lies when our hearts are hungry." Starving for the answer to that internal question, they search externally.

Who are you?

The neurologist, Paul MacLean, suggested that humans have essentially three brains attempting to work as one. The reptilian brain, at the core, is responsible for arousal, homeostasis, and reproduction. The paleomammalian, our old-mammal brain, surrounding it is involved with learning, memory, and emotion. Lastly, the neomammalian, or new-mammal brain, required for conscious thought and self-awareness, sits atop the other two.

The Triune Brain theory suggests that the basal ganglia and a number of the surrounding structures within the base of the forebrain are responsible for 'species-typical' behaviors, which are present in aggression, dominance, territoriality, and ritual displays. This is our reptilian brain. Even though we have evolved beyond what we, *life*, once was, some of our ancestral, primal parts are still being epigenetically expressed. It is a matter of survival and continuity on the primal level. This part of the brain is not actively asking "who am I", but it is gravitating toward what is familiar.

If you have ever left home and arrived at school, your office, or your routine destination without recollection of the commute, it is because your basal ganglia, the place where we accrue defaults and habits, had taken the wheel.

On the old mammalian level, the monkey brain, we begin to find a more definite sense of self. We thumb through our memories, our emotions, our preferences, our abilities, our knowledge for the answer to this question.

"I am a dog person," or "I am a cat person" are attempts to answer this age old question, but you are not your preference for a domesticated pet.

It is a well established idea that a person's favorite word is their name. "I am Matthew Emmorey," is a very appropriate answer to the aforementioned question. But it does not describe me. It is a noise I have a Pavlovian response to. It is another preference. When I die, my headstone will have two dates and a dash. Rest in peace. Matt will be done, dead, and buried. Yet I believe I will live on in Heaven and beyond. "I am Matthew" therefore only encapsulates my mortal components, and I am much more than that.

"I am a graphic designer." What happens when you fall in love with painting? With drawing? With photography? By identifying with your profession, what are you denying yourself? Will you have an identity crisis if you go a year without graphic design? "I am a creative person" is closer, but is still a redundant attempt at answering this question. You are a human being created in God's image, and there is none in the universe more creative than your image-bearer...We are all creative at our core.

Are you your hobbies?

"I am a writer."

"I am a mountain biker."

"I am a climber."

Are we our relationships?

"I am Ralph's wife." This answer hints at an elaborate arranged marriage pre-conception. Were you born to be Ralph's wife? God forbid, if Ralph dies before you, who will you be then?

These are things you do. What you do is more indicative of what you worship than who you are. You are not your hobbies. When the writer, the biker, the climber, or any other hobbyist stops, they continue to exist. These ideas about identity are incomplete. Identification with preference, profession, relationships, hobbies, or deeper more difficult things like shame and trauma are lacking one vital ingredient: *Integrity.*

We are not these things. These are just the things we know, the memories we hold dear, and our emotional reactions to certain stimuli. These are good answers to, "What do I like?" but not to the question, "Who am I?"

On the neomammalian level, the brain responsible for conscious thought and self-awareness, we might be able to sort it out.

All of the previous ideas fall short on the dynamism in the question that includes: *Who are you....always?*

I am.

integrity

Integrity is an inner sense of wholeness. It is derived from qualities such as honesty and consistency of character. Integrity is being the same person no matter where you show up. Your friends, family, significant other, colleagues, and strangers all get versions of you aligned in values and belief.

Each of us has an integrous standard within us. our inner Self is our anchor in Divinity. Our inner Self is unwavering and indistractable. It is honest, accepting, present, grounded, loving, faithful, gentle, patient, trusting, joyful, controlled, and peaceful. It is within reach.

But it has legendary competition. Our duality, by its very name, hints at a lack of integrity. It suggests that it is something inconsistent, set aside, and unpredictable.

"Who am I?" ought to be answered by our inner Self, not by our dualistic nature. Who are you always? From God's knowing, who were you created to be? While we trounce around through life trying on different skins, Self sends emotions through us to indicate our proximity to integrity.

Abraham Hicks calls it *sniffing around*. Where is integrity in this moment?

What action will be the most aligned with who I am? *To thine own Self be true.* We figure that out by sniffing around...

Upon recognition of the two parts of ourselves, the question shifts into: *How can we more consistently operate out of Self?* I want to be in love with my life, in full acceptance and surrender, to be like Josiah's sons leaping in complete trust in their father, to never be held back by small-minded fears, to see myself the way God sees me. More than anything, I do not want to identify with this minute-by-comparison invention that I made for myself. My duality is not me. I am not the reptile, the monkey, or my ego. I wish to be who God has created. I intend for my ego to stay out of the way. *One order of God's plan, please!*

I can be like Thomas, full of doubt. Doubting Thomas asked Jesus: "We do not know where You are going, so how can we know the way?"

Jesus answered, "I am the way and the truth and the life. No one comes to the Father except through Me. If you had known Me, you would know My Father as well. From now on you do know Him and have seen Him."

What Jesus is telling Thomas here is how he can operate out of Divinity. The version of Thomas that God created is not overwhelmed with doubt. His doubt is a Thomas invention. Thomas wavers between trust and doubt, enough that he follows Jesus but consistently expresses doubt in Jesus' decisions. Doubt was Thomas' most available barometer of alignment. Our own duality presents itself in a multitude of ways - but there is only one way to Divinity, to integrity, to Self.

"I am the way and the truth and the life," Jesus said.

Following Christ, indwelling as your highest intuition, is the way to integrity. One follows Him on their knees, humbly, in complete surrender. Integrity is our wholeness. Jesus is the path to wholeness, to goodness, to unification with love. Any version of yourself without Him is not completely expressed.

My priest said, *"You are a good thing in bad condition."* You are Divinity swaddled in duality. The Lord is the mechanic, keen to return you to your factory settings. You have gotten a little beaten up along the way but you're in luck, the Restorer is in and He's been expecting you.

the boy who breaks things

I drove through Lampasas, TX recently and noticed a business called *Absolute Demolition*. It had a nice parking lot, a nice fasade, and decent landscaping. From outside appearances, this business was thriving.

That set me to thinking.

Who is this proprietor? A fellow boy who breaks things, perhaps?

If that's true, at one point in this business owner's life he must have realized that his skills of destruction are not an inherently bad thing. After all, plenty of structures must be absolutely demolished before something can be made anew. I had been beating myself up over a particular characteristic of my history while another person was busy perceiving it as a gift, giving it as a gift, and profiting off of it famously.

In this minor revelation, I felt the Judge within me shift uneasily. Something bubbled to the surface like, *Is that what you want to be? A breaker again?*

"Judge," I addressed him. "Prejudice? *Really?*"

"It's what I do, sir," the Judge responded sheepishly.

By the time I drove by Absolute Demolition, I had not thought of myself as The Boy Who Breaks Things in years. It turns out, guilt can be a close friend to awareness as long as you don't identify with it. In that tear-filled moment on the couch, I allowed myself to be identified with my guilt. It was such a part of me that I condemned myself for it. The Judge Within slammed the gavel and said, "GUILTY!" I dressed myself in stripes, put my undeserving self in shackles, and shut the door of the prison-of-my-own-making behind me.

Forgiveness has been one of the most important concepts in my life. Without forgiveness, my soul would be stained with the prismatic colors of all my transgressions, and all the transgressions of my ancestors. I would still be The Boy Who Breaks Things, the ancestor of Cain, defined by my mistakes. You cannot get out from under the crushing weight of your past without forgiveness.

In Matthew 18:21-22, Peter is wondering about the proper amount of times to offer forgiveness to another. It reads, "Then Peter came up and said to Him, 'Lord, how many times shall my brother sin against me and I still forgive him? Up to seven times?'" Peter had more than doubled the Jewish standard of pardoning someone three times for an offense. "Jesus said to him, 'I do not say to you, up to seven times, but up to seventy times seven times.'"

In other words, *endlessly*. You are forgiven that much. You are called to forgive that much, yourself as often as others.

God says, "You are forgiven! I am not factoring that into how I see you. That is not *You*, per se." Instantaneously, eternally, upon your acceptance.

"What do you mean, *that is not me*? That is me. I did that stuff. I am The Boy Who Breaks Things."

"I forgive you," God said. "Clean slate. Let me help you up. Let me dust you off. There you go, good as new."

The Boy Who Breaks Things is a bit confused by this gesture. "Why are you being so nice to me?" he wants to know. His mind is flipbooking through his life, drawing on memories of selfishness, reckless abandonment, destruction, betrayal...

God sees the boy. God knows the boy. "This is Me, son. This is how I am. I want you to know Me...I *love you*."

The Boy takes a moment to consider His words. "Clean slate?"

God nods.

prodigal sons and daughters

In the parable of the prodigal son, the loving father has two sons. The younger son requests his inheritance early, and his father grants his request. He then goes off into the world wastefully and extravagantly, eventually finding that the ways of living he wanted have left him destitute. Realizing that this squandering way did not lead him to happiness, he must return home empty-handed. He intends to beg his father to accept him back as a servant. To his surprise, he is not scorned by his father but is welcomed back with a celebration. The older son is confused and hurt, and distances himself from the celebration, as he feels his brother's squandering ways are being rewarded.

The loving father explains to him, "You are ever with me, and all that I have is yours, but thy younger brother was lost and now he is found."

I know a few people who identify with the older brother. I know a lot more who identify with the prodigal son.

In the phantom pain of our psyches, we remember what it was like at home, in perfect fellowship with our Father. Yet there is a pervasive other voice that speaks to us through our desires. It urges us to take our birthright - our freewill and individuality - and run with it. We desire to run wild in the world, to satisfy our curiosities, to experience everything, to burn the candle at both ends and to pretend that it will never burn out. We express our sovereignty without reservation, celebrating the idea that we are independent and set aside. We answer to nobody!

Prodigal children, at some point, take stock of their lives. The gifts we had brought from home were not limitless. We had taken them for granted, falsely thinking that we were the Source. We had drawn off them with impunity, with certainty that they would never run out, and when they did...well, we realized that we kind of always knew they would. There was always that phantom pain, the inkling that we once had a connection that was now gone.

That's why we reacted with embarrassment. We knew better. And because of that, we were sure that our mistakes were unforgivable. We were sure that we would never be forgiven, that we would wear our shame around our necks forevermore.

Those of us who turn back to our home and seek a relationship with our Father again find that we are welcome with open arms. We do not have to carry around the weight of past identities. Our loving Father is ready to take guilt off our shoulders. At any moment, we can come home and be well received.

We are the prodigal sons and daughters. Some of us are just leaving home to choose ourselves, others experiencing the delights of squandering, others beginning to feel the error of our ways, others spiritually destitute fearing scorn and punishment. Wherever we are, one thing is for certain: there is a loving, forgiving Father waiting for us at home.

He is forgiving so we will *always* have a chance to know Him.

the truth, the way and the life

Rumi said, "Yesterday I was clever, so I wanted to change the world. Today I am wise, so I am changing myself."

When we love something - *truly love it* - we tend to surround ourselves with it as much as possible. To decorate our walls, we put up our favorite sports teams, actors, musicians, photographs, art or saviors. We get totems tattooed on our skin. Personally, I wear the colors of my beloved Spartans. I stock my fridge with my favorite foods, and my house with my favorite people and animals. I wear a cross around my neck forged from my favorite metals. I write books talking about the ideals I want to surround myself with in the world. When I pray, I pray for faith, for love, for patience. When I give thanks, I am grateful for the presence of my various loves: my family, health, safety, food.

Marie Kondo asks, *Does it spark joy?* to remind us to fill our spaces with things that bring us to life. We often cannot help ourselves from talking about what we love...Why else would parents (pet parents, too) enjoy talking about their children (or pets) so much?

If you want to surround yourself with cleanliness, respect, and responsibility, you might pull off to the side of the road to pick up trash, like my dad did in the story of the stuffed animals.

If you want to surround yourself with passion, you might play a sport, join a club, or immerse yourself into a particular community. You might also be passionate, throwing yourself headlong into your loves and waiting to see who joins you.

If you want to surround yourself with laughter, you might seek out people of good humor, tell a lot of jokes, go to comedy shows, and cultivate a disposition that does not take itself too seriously.

What do you want to surround yourself with?

What if you wanted to surround yourself with abounding and ceaseless Love? What if you wanted the world to know God...like really, actually know Him? You would have noticed how many people had made up their minds about Him after the first snag. You would have noticed how many "Christians" were channeling the table-flipping Jesus without channeling the loving, patient, attentive, listening Jesus. You would have noticed how the exact people who Christ often sought out nowadays feel unwelcome in church. You would have noticed that the behavior of many Christians drowns out the presence of God, instead of making Him easily seen and known. You may have noticed your own hesitation toward identification with Christianity because as you seek to silence your own Judge, you see judgment is such common practice amongst Christians...

Yesterday I was clever...I looked around at the world and saw it needed changing.

Today I see that I am a citizen of the universe. I am not set aside. I am not separate. I do not operate behind a veil of affect. Anything I am, I add to the world. I achieve nothing through negative reinforcement, because the hate with which I meet hate only amplifies hate. The violence with which I thwart violence only teaches violence. I cannot show my heart through my harshness.

"People do not care how much you know until they know how much you care," Theodore Roosevelt said.

In my sales roles, I have heard, "If people like you, they will listen to you. If they listen to you, they will believe you. If they believe you, they will buy from you."

In order to like someone, I have to feel safe around them. Threats don't make me feel safe. Love does. Acceptance does. Understanding does. Everybody is tired of being told they are a bad person. Everyone is tired of being told they are going to hell, lest they repent. Fear does not teach love. Others do not come to know the entirety of Jesus if all we are doing is flipping tables.

The best way to evangelize, according to Hans Urs von Bathasar, is to move from the beautiful to the good to the true. Surround a person with beauty and do your best to *patiently* help them see it. When they do, it will merge with them and open them to the good in themselves. Eventually, they will begin to see the truth.

Perhaps, at some point, it becomes time to flip the table. Up until that point, seek the beautiful direction. If it is not immediately apparent, stand still. Find it, merge with it, and then share it.

Jesus loved to be with His Father. He wanted to teach the world to know Him. He wanted to be surrounded by God. He saw how ineffective it would be to free the Hebrews from Roman domination by destroying them. One does not fill the world with Love by warmongering.

Through His life, Jesus lived instructions on how to get to know God. Thomas told him, "Lord, we don't know where you are going, so how can we know the way?" Jesus then explained to Thomas what it meant to follow Him. When Jesus said, "I am the way and the truth and the life," He was helping Thomas recall the memory of Divinity, so he could identify contrast to it. He was not saying "*Follow me!*" for his own benefit, although it is natural for us to project our own egos onto the situation. Jesus was helping Thomas identify the Path. When Thomas, or anyone, asks themself "*What Path am I on?*", they can know the answer for Christ provides the true north for our internal compasses to navigate by.

Albeit, even before He walked the Earth, the North Star always existed. I told my priest, "It seems unfair to early Hebrews who lived before Jesus… They didn't have Him to follow." My priest answered beautifully. "You misunderstand. They, too, had access to Jesus. Not as a living example but in the calm of their minds."

In the famous sermon on the mount, Jesus spoke out of an overflow. He wanted to change the world. So, to a multitude of clever people, he shared the wisdom of how these people could change themselves. He loved them, and so he gave them instructions on how to be less *of the world*, and more of their Creator. If Jesus' life alone is not enough of an example of the way, the truth and the life, then the ideals within this sermon ought to color in the blanks. Because Jesus lived beautifully, the words of goodness and truth resonated with authenticity.

the sermon on the mount

If religious language puts you off, this coming section will provide triggers. I encourage you to read, nonetheless, and make note of the passages that turn you away.

This is a radical sermon. It can feel idealistic and unrealistic. Because it is Jesus speaking through a Christian text, it has Christian conformity, and the lessons are spoken in a lexicon that is not relatable to everyone. For this lack of affinity, the words may appear harsh and unloving. They may seem preachy, because they are Christ preaching. They may feel unattainable, and if that is the case, I believe reactions of unattainability are not beside the point. In this way, we are shown a high standard that cannot be reached without surrendering to a higher power.

I include this section to showcase the teachings of Christ Jesus, the world's highest vibrational guru. It ought to be overlaid and compared against the Eightfold Path as taught by Buddha or the lessons of Lord Krishna in Bhagavad Gita. Remember, the lessons of these guides were delivered to a group of people with a particular set of worldly challenges, cultural norms, and vocabularic affinity. Try to extract the lesson without being lost in the word choices. They are attempts to express ineffable Divinity in familiar language.

Now when Jesus saw the crowds, he went up on a mountainside and sat down. His disciples came to him, and he began to teach them.

The Beatitudes

He said:

3 "Blessed are the poor in spirit, for theirs is the kingdom of heaven. 4 Blessed are those who mourn, for they will be comforted. 5 Blessed are the meek, for they will inherit the earth. 6 Blessed are those who hunger and thirst for righteousness, for they will be filled. 7 Blessed are the merciful, for they will be shown mercy. 8 Blessed are the pure in heart, for they will see God. 9 Blessed are the peacemakers, for they will be called children of God. 10 Blessed are those who are persecuted because of righteousness, for theirs is the kingdom of heaven.

11 "Blessed are you when people insult you, persecute you and falsely say all kinds of evil against you because of me. 12 Rejoice and be glad, because great is your reward in heaven, for in the same way they persecuted the prophets who were before you.

The Beatitudes account for only a tenth of the sermon. Verses 13-111 can be found in APPENDIX B (p. 250).

what does this mean?

There are entire books breaking down this 111 verse sermon.

The values in this sermon were as radical two-thousand years ago as they are today. The imploring of being *in the world but not of the world* was just as relevant then. There are many misguided ways that have been normalized. Some of the destruction to our souls is celebrated, and so we invite it upon ourselves with open arms. Without discernment, many travel the wide, crowded path to destruction. Many get swept up in a deluge of default.

The sermon holds instructions to cultivate an internal environment rich with Love and unity. For the person who can *unidentify* with their duality, these are instructions toward living as God has created you to be. It is about extending your awareness beyond your own smallness. The resistance we feel toward certain precepts in this sermon are areas where we have become conditioned to be *of the world*.

If these ideas scare you, or make you feel hopeless to achieve this state on your own, you are not wrong. The standard is placed out in front of us in the form of Jesus to teach us God's nature. The standard Jesus implores us to live by is not possible by our own volition, yet he implores us to live it nonetheless. All of this is to show us what it means to be human, to become aware of our nature, to not feel guilty about it but to seek a higher authority to surrender to. We were never meant to do life alone. The world is not on our shoulders, but some of us try to take it all upon ourselves.

A pessimist will look at the world and see man's sin nature. They do not believe that we will ever overcome our own selfish desires in favor of a grand, unified vision. They become sure that humans are champions of waste and destruction. They believe that salvation is something we must accomplish for ourselves. A pessimist has become aware of the need, but not yet aware of the Loving Solution. Because they see a troubled world, it is hard for pessimists to believe in a loving Father. However, if life gets hard when we turn away from Love, it is not evidence of a cruel creator but of a misguided turn on our part.

Here is my summation of Jesus's instructions on turning back:

1. Vulnerability is strength. Vulnerability is leaving yourself open to attack. Beneath the act of vulnerability is trust. It requires trust in your fellow man. It requires trust that everything will be okay, despite acknowledging that it is not okay right now. Vulnerability is the first step in encouraging your awareness beyond yourself. In order to create a world where you can trust people, you must encourage them to be trustworthy by first trusting them.

2. Open your heart and keep it open. The brave soul who loves unconditionally will find great comfort.

3. Be quick to admit your mistakes and make reconciliations.

4. Remove violence from your mind. The violence we inflict upon others is first inflicted within ourselves. In order to act violently, first we need to project aggression onto the world. This creates an aggressive internal state. Violence is not our right mind.

5. Seek loving solutions. Our identifying egos have created an illusion of separation between us, yet we are all members of one body. Love helps us *remember*. Anything else mutates and magnifies separation.

6. Love is such a powerful force that it threatens false authority. The loving one will be questioned, called names, misunderstood, and persecuted. Such rejection will be done by the fearful, the wounded, and the small-minded. Keep loving in spite of the hurt they wield. In these moments, remember the invulnerability of Self and love them.

7. There is a paradox of identity. As you surrender your own ideas of your individuality, your created Self will be magnified. When you die to yourself today, your ego starves, and you become free to exhibit all the uniqueness God has created in you.

8. One cannot simultaneously seek recognition for their righteousness and be righteous. It is the ego who desires accolades. To the Self, connection to our Father is reward enough. Keep this in mind in charity, prayer, fasting, and otherwise.

9. The Self is invulnerable. One does not need to protect what is invulnerable. Therefore, wrath and violence are ego thoughts of weakness. Wrath and violence project themselves onto the world and then destroy from the inside. They are like the acid that destroys the container.

10. Once you comprehend your invulnerability, vulnerability will feel like authenticity.

11. One's value is not retained in the variable flesh, but in the immutable soul.

12. Lust blinds your heart. Lust clouds your purity.

13. Your word carries all the weight it needs. "Yes" and "no" are enough. You do not need to swear any oaths. You do not need to defend or explain yourself. If you are doing what you believe is right, it does not need to make sense to anyone else.

14. The temptation to justify yourself can be a strong indication of your ego's involvement. "Yes, I closed my heart, *but...*" means the necessary work lies within *you.* Tend to the weeds in your own garden.

15. Love your enemies until you have no enemies. Always seek first to understand. Know your tendency to fear what you do not know. Compassion is the skin of understanding. However, even if understanding is elusive, lead with compassion in the meantime.

16. Your ego and your Self have contradictory motives. You cannot satisfy both. Your Self will lead you to treasures in heaven and on earth. Your ego will lead you to neither.

17. The past and the future are your greatest obstacles to God. Within the present moment you will find everything that you need. Rest assured that the same will be true of the present moments you meet tomorrow.

18. Your Judge measures *you* with the same stick it measures others.

19. Innocence cannot project.

20. If you are clear about what you want, and you maintain no contradictions, your Father will delight in gifting it to you. Ask and you shall receive as much as you are aligned with. To ask for great gifts of your Father is a testament to your great faith in Him. The inverse is also true. However, you cannot receive what you are simultaneously rejecting.

21. You will know the quality of a thing by the quality of its fruits. Above judgment is recognition. Recognition is a power of awareness, not of judgment.

22. The Truth needs no defense. A wise person builds their life upon sturdy, resolute foundations.

part three
willpower

the road to permanence part 3/4

Apeninom picked up the phone.

"Hey, are you still selling your mattress and bed frame?"

Apenimon was. His new bedroom in his new house was large enough for a king-size bed. The man's new ideology included making space for the things he wanted to accommodate into his life. His house was large enough for a family that did not exist yet, and he thought it made sense to buy a bed that could accommodate a partner he knew was around the corner.

The elderly woman on the phone asked, "I just moved to the area. I don't know anyone and I don't have an SUV. Can you deliver?"

"I can. Do you want to look at the stuff first before I bring it over? Any chance you could come by the house?" Apenimon asked. He had a lot of interested buyers in his old stuff. He felt a strong desire to serve this woman well, even if it meant making a little less money.

Later that afternoon, the woman arrived. She had a hundred questions, but Apenimon answered them patiently. After all her questions, she was ready to move forward. Apenimon loaded the bed frame and mattress into the car.

"Just follow me over to my house," the woman said. "It's not far."

Twenty-five minutes later, Apenimon was weaving in-and-out of traffic trying to keep up with the woman's erratic driving. Not only was she difficult to follow, but her house was not around the corner. A surge of regret was steaming up inside of him. *Why didn't I just sell this to someone who could pick it up?* He had a busy afternoon.

Once to the woman's house, as Apenimon was unloading the bed frame, the woman changed her mind. "I think I only want to buy the mattress," she said.

"I am selling the set," Apenimon said. He heard the frustration in his voice, but he hoped the woman would not.

"*Oh*," she said. "Well I just need the bed frame. I already have one, and I should save my money. Will you take $40 for just the mattress?"

A slew of curses crossed Apenimon's mind. *I just drove thirty minutes!* Quickly, in an attempt to salvage the situation, Apenimon reached out to another potential buyer. "Would you be interested in the bed frame only?" he asked.

"No, I want the set," the man said.

A couple of different ideas entered Apenimon's mind. He could charge the woman a delivery fee to compensate him for his time. He could just say no to her new proposal, and go sell the set to someone else. He could chastise her for wasting his time, tell her how disrespectful that was, and peel out. He sure wanted to.

Instead, he found himself saying, "$40 is fine." *I am just going to love this woman*, Apenimon thought. *I don't want to be rude to her.* He actually did, but he knew he would regret it later. However, he had a bunch of irritated, annoyed energy that he needed to do something with. He decided to channel it into assisting the woman further. *I am going to murder her with kindness*, Apenimon thought. "Here, let me carry that in for you."

When he hauled the mattress into the bedroom, he found the woman taking the sheets off of her old mattress. He said, "I thought you just moved here?"

"A couple months ago."

"Already getting a new mattress?" he asked.

"This one is too firm."

"It looks new," Apenimon said. "Would you like me to haul it away for you?"

"You would do that?" the elderly woman said.

"It's gotta go," he said matter-of-factly.

The woman was over the moon. While Apenimon hauled her old mattress to his truck, the woman made him a cold beverage. When he came back inside to collect the money, she asked him, "Do you have a need for an old italian leather purse? I don't know why you would, but you have been so kind to me and I want to give you something extra."

"I can find a home for that, too," Apenimon said smiling. He took the money, the water, the purse, and thanked the woman. Before he drove away, he made a quick phone call to the prospective buyer. "I am on the way with the bed frame and the mattress. I will be at your place in 15 minutes."

✦   ✦   ✦

Your mind goes where you will it. It does not force you to think about anything. If you wish, right now you could think about a purple duck. Your mind will conjure up an image of a purple duck. I bet it's quacktastic. Whatever you will your mind to contemplate, it will.

The mind, however, is notoriously bad at understanding negatives. *Don't think about a purple duck.* By the time you understand the directive, your mind has already conjured up a purple duck.

An old boss of mine in the hospitality industry had to continuously remind me to offer the guests positive statements, instead of double negatives. She wanted me to say "my pleasure" instead of "no problem" to guests. Even spoken cheerfully, she explained, all the guest's mind hears is "*no*" and "*problem*".

If I did not want you to think about a purple duck, I would not have said, "Don't think about a purple duck". I would have instructed you to think about something else entirely. In this way, I would have almost guaranteed that you would not have randomly landed on a purple duck.

What do you want in your life?

"Well, I don't want to be sad anymore."

"I don't want my boss to keep passing me up for promotions."

"I don't want to struggle with money anymore."

"I don't want to be alone."

A lot of the time we answer questions about what we want in this life with what we do not want. Our subconscious mind is always listening. It does not know what to make of these sorts of wishes. It hears: "sad", "pass me up for promotion", "struggle with money" and "be alone". The negatives are subtracted from the wish, and you are left receiving exactly what you do not want.

When Jesus arrived at the well with the Samaritan woman, he said, "Will you give me a drink?"

He did not say, "I don't want to be thirsty anymore."

You will your mind, and the universe in turn, through positive statements. Be wary of *want-energy*. I mentioned in a previous chapter that the wanting mind fixates on lack. "I *want*" something tacitly implies its absence. "*I desire*" is a charge of energy. Desires do not have to be attached to anything in particular. You ride a desire like a wave. I have used the language "I wish" over "I desire" in the upcoming examples for no particular reason. The secret is maintaining the knowledge that nothing is lacking in your life. When you wish for something, maintain that it is already here. Go forward carrying the energy of the wish as if it were granted the moment it was made. The universe operates at a slight delay, but maintain the fulfillment of the wish in your energy, and *it will* materialize.

What do you want in your life?

"I wish to be bliss of the blissful." Pick up bliss and carry it.

"I wish to be promoted." You already are. Act as if. The upleveling will happen with you, and later the title will come. Give the world a chance to respond to your new character.

"I wish to experience financial abundance." Attune to it now and the money will follow suit.

"I wish for my cherished life partner." Cultivate conditions where he or she will thrive. Be the tropics to her rosemallow. Create the space that they can flow easily into. Like Apenimon did, buy the house with extra bedrooms, the bed with extra space, or whatever comes up as you embody the corresponding energy.

Your mind is at your service. The universe is powerless to resist what your mind continually conceives. Whatever limitations you believe in your mind *will* be proven out in the universe. Watch all of your beliefs as they materialize in front of you. This can be the most empowering truth to embody, or the most devastating reality if ignored.

"Ask, and it will be given to you" is a beautiful, potent fact. Therefore, you must be disciplined about what and how you ask the universe for things.

"I don't want to be taken advantage of," you tell yourself. Your subconscious hears *"be taken advantage of"*. The next time somebody expresses their problem that needs solving to you, your subconscious has already been conditioned with a subtle directive. You decide to help them, but God forbid, you don't want to be taken advantage of. After the favor has concluded, you are waiting for the universe to respond to your request. Once enough time has passed, you realize that no thanks or reciprocation is coming. Once again, your kindness was taken advantage of. Not only that, you have opened the door to a victim mentality.

Imagine the powerful difference if your self-talk became, "I will be appreciated." There is a stark absence of any victimhood, there is clear empowerment, solid intentionality, and above all, you get to choose what feels like appreciation. The next time someone expresses their problem, how do you respond differently? *You will be appreciated*, you remind yourself. The ball is in your court. Perhaps you decide not to solve this person's problem, but you are clear on what is important to you. Perhaps you set clear boundaries. Perhaps you come to agreeable terms ahead of time, so the loving solution is mutually beneficial.

It is one thing to know you can *will your mind*. It is another thing to know how to will your mind effectively. When you effectively will your mind, you make reality. You manipulate the universe. You take advantage of the complete sovereignty of your own experience. There is nobody that can cross your boundaries. There is nobody that can make you feel anything. There is nobody who can do anything to you to gain control of you. When we are the captains of our willpower, our environments both internal and external are under the control of our thoughts. Nobody can will your thoughts but you.

the power of clarity

Your heart and mind are powerful spellcasters.

Your thoughts are spells.

Spells are more commonly thought of as spoken words, but words are only powerful when they are aligned with thoughts. A word spoken out of alignment with your heart is barely a wisp of wind.

I have been called nasty names and felt loved. Sometimes the worst words become terms of endearment. I have no fear of words. Words cannot hurt us. The reason Jesus was The Word was because he embodied it. He *thought* it. He lived it. He did not merely speak it. His heart and His mind and His thoughts were aligned with His words, and so the words appeared powerful. Miracles are performed when they are embodied, not simply spoken.

To embody a wish is to know it is already granted. "Ask, and it *shall be given* to you; seek, and you *shall* find; knock, and it *shall* be opened to you." If you are tempted to put this to the test, remember to introduce faith into the matrix. Upon accepting this statement as fact, you have prepared yourself to receive.

My friend Crystal Harrell, the best-selling author of the book *Crystal Clear*, who has spoken at Les Brown summits, who exchanges letters with Dr. Ben Carson, who is regularly experiencing realities that at times she could only dare to dream, had a profound realization early in life. She wrote, "I realized that everything I needed was already here *but me.*"

What good is co-creation if you reject the blessing in the form it has materialized?

What good is wishing, praying, and riding desire without the faith that God is in the business of providing?

Everything you need is already here. If you feel a lack, come back.

Back in February of 2021, I conducted an unexpected experiment. My friend introduced me to his pendulum, which is an obelisk of conductive metal that dangles on a metallic chord. One uses a pendulum to divine truth. I was skeptical then, and even after witnessing this device in action, I am still trying to debunk the phenomenon. To use a pendulum, you or a companion will dangle it out in front of your body and speak to it. I am not completely certain how it works, but I can reason that it responds to subtle fluctuations in your energetic field. There is another method of muscle testing using kinesiology that can also be used to calibrate truth. I suspect these methodologies are all being informed from the same quantum source.

Your brain and your heart produce an electromagnetic pulse. When you tell a truth, your body resonates with that truth. When you lie, your body responds differently to that falsehood. Think of a lie detector test. The electrodes are responding to an elevated heart rate, whereby any stark irregularity is indicative of a fib. A lie is less easy to live in than the truth. There is a measurable vibrational delta between the two.

JORDAN PETERSON SAID,

"To tell the truth is to bring about the most
habitable reality into Being."

I repeated to the pendulum, "My name is Matt" until the obelisk began to sway forward and back. After about 30 seconds of this, I switched to repeating, "My name is Matthew." The pendulum amazingly responded. Instead of nodding back and forth, it began to swing in a neat circle. Wanting conclusive answers, I switched to, "My name is Matt." It went back to nodding. Then I tried, "My name is Bob" several times. It continued nodding. When I returned to, "My name is Matthew" the circular motion returned. I tried this for 10 minutes with amazement.

quantum clarity

Interestingly, your heart is 60 times stronger than your brain electrically and 100 times stronger than your brain magnetically. Now consider the potency of a prayer aligned with your heart. God is so eager to see our heart's desires fulfilled that He has created a universe whose mechanics responds diligently to it. The mechanics may function indifferently according to the programming, but God is working with you and through you for the fulfillment of mankind.

My given name is Matthew, but I have always gone by Matt. Only over the past couple years have a few important people in my life begun calling me Matthew. The way my energy responded to my given name over my nickname and a fake name left an impression. It showed me how powerful my body is electromagnetically when aligned with truth. It is enough to shift the fabric of the universe in front of me.

A request that is backed by your heart is destined to be fulfilled, so long as you are prepared to receive.

I am continuously identifying cognitive dissonance within my belief system. There are plenty of contradictions yet to untangle. I know, right now, outside of my awareness I have things that I am wishing for that I am also blocking. Such as, "God, I desire a family" and "God, thank you for these spectacular mornings of peace and solitude." Both of these wishes exist to some extent inside of me. God is waiting inside the vibrational reality of both of these desires with His gift, but I do not show up at either one consistently enough to receive.

What the mind conceives and the heart uniformly desires will be received. How beautiful is it that the universe responds to our hearts? Built into the mechanics of the universe is the reliable fulfillment of the wishes of our deepest alignment. God has implanted a divining organ within our chests. Think of your heart like a compass attuned to True North, your *north star*, self-actualization, your divine purpose. It ought to be great news that what you're meant for will be steeped in love.

My therapist often says, "God does not put a desire in your heart that He does not intend to fulfill."

Crystal wrote, "I realized that everything I needed was already here *but me.*"

So the challenge becomes identifying the contradictions in our hearts. When there are no contradictions, the universe bends and warps and wiggles to bring you what you wish. When there are contradictions, what is the world to do but try to respond to both only to have them cancel each other out? You become like a recipient with your arms out but your hands clenched in fists.

Perhaps you have to do what I did, to prove this truth to myself.

I learned an equation that was helping people effectively manifest: Desire + Expectation = Materialization. Another way to say this is Prayer + Faith = Receive. Recognizing the abundance of the world, this is about getting clear on your desires and then keeping a keen lookout for them trying to present themselves.

the baseball

My dad came down to visit me in Texas. Over the years, he has instilled within me a love of baseball, and so while he was here I bought us tickets to a UT Longhorns game.

I decided to start small. I wanted to prove the mechanism of predictable manifestation on something I knew I would not actively be contradicting.

As we sat down in our seats along the first baseline, I said to him, "Dad, by the end of this weekend I will hold a baseball in my hand, I will look over at you, and I will say, 'See, I told you I would get a baseball.'" He laughed, probably a bit unsure about what I was up to. A couple hits later, a foul ball was struck down the first base line. It bounced about fifteen feet from us. It was rolling toward another group of fans. I could have jumped up and gotten the baseball, but I remained glued in my seat.

In the minutes after the baseball was grabbed by another fan, I realized something. I had an attachment to *how* this baseball needed to arrive. I was attached to the idea that this baseball would appear in my hand through no effort of my own. If I scrambled to my feet, if I ran down the aisle and fought another fan for the baseball, this is not proof of the right thing. This might prove I am faster, stronger, or better at predicting the location of foul balls than other spectators, but it would not prove that desire plus expectation equals manifestation.

My dad, a pragmatic farmer's son turned practical mechanical engineer, would not have his worldview shifted by something he has experienced countless times in his life. *Cool, you went to the baseball game and fought a kid for a baseball.* This proves nothing about the majesty of our fantastic universe.

In order for this experiment to prove anything, the baseball had to come into my possession *differently*. I think I would have allowed standing up and catching it, if it was hit my way, but it absolutely had to *come to me*.

Nine innings came and went. No baseball.

I reflected on what I had said to my dad: "By the end of this weekend..." After the game, I did not let my Dad forget about the assignment. I walked with the nonchalant confidence of a man who believed. And I really did. The stakes were pretty low, so my confidence was tethered to the humor of the experiment. Plus, Dad was bought in. He said, "Okay, by the end of the weekend you are going to hold a baseball, you are going to look up at me and say, 'Dad, see, I told you I would get a baseball.'" *Exactly.*

Later that night, the two of us were capping off a legendary father-son Saturday by watching *The Patriot*. It was about 8:00pm, golden hour. All of the sudden, the sun beamed through the clouds and lit up my balcony. I paused the movie and asked my dad, "Do you want to go for a little sunset walk?"

We walked up the hill to a view overlooking Austin. The park was empty but for a man playing with his dog. We sat down to take in the sunset. After sitting there for a couple minutes, the dog ran over to greet us. It turned out the dog wanted us to join in on his game of fetch. Into my outstretched hand, the dog dropped a slobbery baseball.

I just looked at my dad and laughed.

Desire + Expectation.

So was born the *Manifestation Game*.

the yellow shovel

I sat at breakfast with one of my fraternity brothers, named Victor. He had come to town for a biomechanics conference. Here we sipped coffee, idly chatting about our lives. He told me about the approaching three-year anniversary of his sobriety. I told him about the baseball and the manifestation game. Talking about sobriety and manifestation dovetailed into a discussion on "point of attraction".

Point of attraction is an idea borne out of some people being much "luckier" than others. I have heard Abraham Hicks use this phrasing to describe *the potency of the effect of one's willpower on the world.* In other words, how effective one is at manifesting.

A sober vessel, a crystal clear mind, takes nearly the entire power of will and focus and concentrates it into a point - a focal point. That focal point becomes a dense singularity. That single concentration is highly effective in manifestation, especially when it is conditioned in conjunction with one's heart. For example, a mind and heart clearly and adroitly fixated on connection will find countless opportunities to connect.

I said to Victor, "Take twenty seconds to cultivate a desire to see a particular object. God is our ultimate teammate in this. If you can unequivocally believe He will bring this object across your path, and you maintain the charge of your desire to see it, you will see it. That's a fact."

Vic said, "I am going for a red dog." He closed his eyes and was silent for half a minute.

I thought, "*Okay, we're in Austin… There are probably 100 dogs on South Congress right now. I bet 25 of them are red…*" but despite my thoughts, I did not rain on his parade. Sure enough, about fifteen seconds later, someone walked by with a rhodesian ridgeback.

I told him, "I am going for a yellow shovel."

"The beauty of this game," he said, "is the yellow shovel might not appear the way you think. It could be a yellow gardening shovel, sure. Or it could be a little sand shovel. Or a painting. Or a picture. Or…I suppose it could be a CAT backhoe."

"*A CAT backhoe,*" I repeated. There was a construction site just down the street but it was too far to see. "I better keep my eyes peeled."

Perhaps Vic's point of attraction was stronger than mine. Fifteen seconds went by and I did not see any yellow shovels. Perhaps I had selected something that God planned to reveal a bit more extravagantly.

The next day, I woke up in a tent at Schafer Bend on a friends' camping trip. The night before we had partied late into the night and had used up our firewood. The girls took the truck to the convenience store nearby, while the boys played spikeball.

After an hour and a few rounds of spikeball, the girls returned. There was an exuberant reunion between one of my friends and an unfamiliar fellow who had returned with the girls. It went something like this:

"Ben?" my friend said.

"Logan!" Ben greeted him.

"How are you here?" They laughed and embraced.

"Craziest thing," Ben said. "I am roadtripping back from California to

South Carolina right now in my truck. I stopped off to get gas and saw your white truck. I thought, 'That looks a bit like Logan's truck. Logan lives a couple hours from here.' And then I saw a blonde girl jump out and I thought, 'That looks a bit like Katelyn.' And then she turned and it was! She was like, 'Ben?'"

Logan asked, "Do you want to camp with us?"

"Yes! I am kinda burned out from driving and was just starting to look for a place to relax in Texas today."

"Ben!" Logan said again with surprise.

"What *impeccable* timing," Ben said. The two friends embraced again.

A little later, everyone was being introduced around the campfire. I shook Ben's hand and gestured toward his truck. "Great rig," I said. It was an older model with a cozy camp setup in the bed beneath the topper. Strapped to the roof rack was a Thule, some gear, and *wouldn't ya know it*, a shovel with a long, yellow handle.

"I just got that shovel," Ben explained when I told him about the game. "As I was heading out from California, someone told me of heavy snow in the mountains. They instructed me not to try to pass the mountains without a shovel in case I got stuck and needed to dig myself out. Guess what: I got stuck and needed to dig myself out. That shovel was a godsend."

CHAPTER 3.4

the blue bouncy ball

After locating the yellow shovel, I immediately set a new target: *A blue bouncy ball*. It was just a random color and the first random object that popped into my mind. It fit my criteria.

I was riding the high of the yellow shovel like God and I had an inside joke. I half expected to be walking down the street and to hear a *BOING...BOING...*and to catch a blue bouncy ball out of midair. I kept a lookout for it. My head was on a swivel - as I walked into coffee shops, into the grocery store, at the park. If I was on a road with a hill, I thought, "*God, I know some kid just dropped a quarter into the vending machine. I know the boy is clumsy. Let the bouncy ball jump awkwardly off a crack, out of his hand, and come bounding my way. I am ready.*" I might have dropped down into the fielding position my dad taught me years before as my baseball coach. *I might have.*

My expectation and my desire were off the charts.

But a month came and went. No blue bouncy ball.

I told my friend, "Something is off with my point of attraction. I can't manifest for shit."

I remembered the conversation I had with Victor about things arriving in a different form than expected. I wracked my brain for what other form a blue bouncy ball might come in. I came up empty handed. "A blue bouncy ball is *a blue bouncy ball*," I thought. I inspected what I expected. I deeply contemplated my psyche and whether or not I had any unconscious attachments. I could find no way around the fact that a blue bouncy ball could come in no other form besides a bouncy ball that is blue...

Another two weeks went by. I was dejected. I was thinking of other things besides blue bouncy balls, I assure you, but it seemed somewhere along the way I had lost something. My focus? My faith? My humility and thereby some connection to God? My potent point of attraction? I don't know. *Something was missing.*

One afternoon I am sitting on my couch. I had just come in from outside. My dog was tossing something around in the yard to himself. What was it? I jumped off the couch and ran out to where he was. Lying on the ground was a blue bouncy ball. It was not a conventional solid blue ball. It was a partially-clear-blue-marble-orb with a flashing LED inside. When it bounced, it glowed. It was so much better and cooler than the blue bouncy ball I had been imagining all along. I found it!

It was in my possession the entire time.

When I had moved into that house a couple months prior, I had brought it with me. It was in a bin with all the dog toys. At some point, I had thrown it for my husky and forgot about it...

It was a relatively mundane possession, but also, despite my attempts not to, I still had become attached to an image of a particular blue bouncy ball. *How much variability could there be?!* Part of that was wrapped up in how the bouncy ball would come into my life, too. It was going to bounce in, with grandeur, out of the clear blue, dramatically and with a story attached.

Of course, notions of romantic resplendence in my life were not limited to the Manifestation Game.

Around the same time of life, I had been trying feverishly to get over an ex.

While there was momentum in my life away from my relationship with her, I had not found a good way to relinquish the attachment I had to her. My identity was so wrapped up in her for so many years that a correction was not happening overnight.

I was doing my best to nurture my new relationship with Bella, but I was not doing a great job. Bella was patient, kind, generous, and understanding. She had been a secure fixture in my life for a year. As I floundered and faltered and screwed up, she was understandably flustered, but resolute. She stuck around.

As I held this glowing, ornate, decadent blue bouncy ball in my hand, I realized something...

Sometimes the things we are waiting for are right in front of us. We cannot seem to take notice because of our attachments to how things need to be. Everything you have been asking for, praying for, strongly desiring for can be right in front of you but you miss it. Even when you inspect what you expect, when you try to get to the core of why something feels like it is missing, the truth is *nothing is missing*. The truth is you have an attachment. It is something you are struggling to let go of. Or, you are waiting for a big, glowing sign with an arrow, attached to the idea of how something will come, what it will look like, what it will feel like. You don't want to change, I get it, because that attachment is a form of security.

discovery and definition

There are two phases to life: discovery and definition. Once a thing is defined, it is our human nature to want to keep it defined. Definition in our life, like our identities, give us solid ideas about who we are and where we fit. Discovery on the other hand, while exciting and mysterious, can become wearisome when you look in the wrong places. Discovery is the counterpart to definition. For some, the sheer act of discovery maintains the purpose of eventual definition. That river flows one way - from discovery to definition. It is genuinely hard to reverse definition and return to discovery. It is hard to *unidentify.*

I believe it is healthy to live in a perpetual state of discovery. Here you are always learning about yourself. Here you have never identified with anything. Definition is predicated by a certain window of time. If you define your existence by the ninety years you spend as a human, that is incomplete. We spoke of this in the previous chapter on identity. Your soul goes on. "*I am*" is still true after you pass away. Your definition of yourself in those ninety years is now obsolete. Why not resist the inclination to define yourself entirely? Sometimes reality is ineffable, and to try to define something would force it to shrink to the size of an imperfect language.

Buddhism teaches that not all suffering is from attachment, but all attachment leads to suffering. My attachment to old ideas of my life's direction was creating suffering for me and the people closest to me.

Everything you have been praying for can be right in front of you, but your attachments are blinding. The best way to manifest your dreams is with the charge of desire, the knowledge of fulfillment, and a disposition of non-attachment to the form it will come about.

Such is the lesson of the blue bouncy ball.

the fridge painting

The manifestation game is full of lessons. Whatever is hindering your point of attraction can be immediately addressed. If you are trying to manifest something using the simple recipe: desire + expectation = result, and it is not working, you really only have a couple ingredients to analyze.

Perhaps it is not the charge of desire that you are playing with. Perhaps you have mistaken desire for want, and you are walking around embodying lack. Because when you want something, what is cleverly disguised in that want is absence. Absence cannot coexist with expectation.

Desire will feel like a charge. It will energize you. The idea will thrill you. If you have ever driven or ridden in a powerful sports car, you will remember the sensation of the car springing to life. You will remember that g-force pressing your back in your seat. You will remember the skip of your heart. There is a feeling, a sort of *"oh shit"* moment, where a big smile spreads across your face and you embrace it. You become one with the power. That is what desire feels like. You could laugh. You could smile. You could cry! Desire is not attached to anything in particular. It is merely an energy of excitement. It is something to ride, not something to cling to.

When I first graduated college and was earning a decent paycheck, my lifestyle remained pretty similar except I began eating differently. Way differently. I bought *The Joy of Cooking* volume 1, and I cooked my way through it. *The more I cooked the more I liked to cook.* I went from being empty-fridge poor to full-fridge wealthy overnight. That was what mattered to me. If I had enough money to fill my fridge with all my favorite foods, I was rich. The days of pulling popcorn bags out of the trashcan at the movies, tearing a hole in the bottom of the bag, and then going to the concession counter for a free refill were over. Hopefully. All I needed to feel like I was secure was a full fridge. My mom always kept the fridge stocked to the light bulb. A full fridge is a little slice of a worryless home.

All that to say, full fridge energy is a vibe for me. It carries safety and security. It also carries artistry, delight, intrigue, enticement, sensation, and anticipation. One way for me to cultivate this energy is to go to the grocery store, load up a cart and fill my fridge with all the delicacies. Another way to cultivate this energy is with intentional gratitude. When I look around my life and actively appreciate things, full fridge energy is released.

Full fridge energy feels like abundance.

While it is and always will be attached to a full fridge, it is also unencumbered by the condition of my refrigerator. There has always been an abundance of goodness and freshness in my life. For the last decade, every new year has been the best year of my life, even when that year has been categorically challenging. Despite all, there has always been plenty in my life to appreciate. I have always had enough to channel full fridge energy. I just have to open the door and shine the Light on it.

One day I opened the fridge and it was especially glorious. My beverage shelf was overflowing with coconut water, smoothies, juices, kombuchas, milks, creams, beers, yogurts, and kefirs. There was bacon, salmon, chicken, ground beef, and crab cakes. There was chocolate, caramels, cakes, and cheeses. When I opened the door, it was like a music box, and out came the glittery tune of "My Favorite Things" from *The Sound of Music*. There were times while working through *The Joy of Cooking* when there really were crisp apple strudels and schnitzel with noodles...

I decided on this day that I wanted a painting of my full fridge. A couple weeks prior I had gone to a podcast recording and met a local artist. I immediately texted her to get the ball rolling. I said, "I don't know if you do commissioned works, but I just had a great idea and I think you would be the perfect artist for it."

She responded, "I am not taking any commissions right now."

I said, "Okay, no worries. Anyway, here's the idea." I sent her a picture of my full fridge and added, "Is there anything more beautiful?"

She laughed. A day later, she messaged me, "I just had a great idea."

"Go on," I responded.

She said, "I don't want to tell ya cause if it sucks then you'll be disappointed." In a second message she said, "But I have an idea and it seems cool in my head, so please hold."

I did not know exactly what to make of that. I scrolled up in our messages and clearly read: "I am not taking any commissions right now." Yet her cryptic message seemed to imply that she was on the job. I left it alone for a couple hours. I figured she would reveal her hidden meaning. But hours turned to days and I still had not heard anything. I was serious about getting the painting done, and if it was not going to be taken on by Sarah, then I wanted to find a new artist. Eventually my curiosity got the best of me.

I messaged her. "Talk about suspense."

Nothing.

A week or so later I said, "So, how is the random possibly-happening-possibly-not-happening surprise coming along?"

She said, "The fridge painting? I forgot about it. But it could happen very easily."

"I was thinking it would make for great kitchen art. How can I support you in this magnificent endeavor?" I said.

She said, "Okay, realistically it sounds like it would be a commission."

I thought, *yeah...*

And then we dove into the brass tax. I never hired a painter before. I did not have any idea how expensive, or how affordable, commissioned art would be. However, when Sarah and I finally settled on the size, I crunched the numbers based on what she charges per square inch. The price was a bit more than I was expecting. Food aside, I have always been pretty frugal. I was riding the charge of desire for this painting, in love with the idea, but extremely unsure if spending $1,200 on a painting was in my budget.

I told Sarah I would pay the first half on the 15th, per her process. On the 20th, I reached out to tell her I was still interested in the painting but needed to figure out the timing.

She said, "No worries! Everything will unfold in its proper timing."

A few more days went by. I was doing what I had seen so many people do around large expenses. They allow themselves time to talk themselves out of it. I knew I wanted it. I knew I could afford it. I knew it would bring me joy. It represented an energy that had carried me far in life. In its own weird way, it was an investment in myself.

But still I floundered.

And then a series of synchronicities arose that could not be ignored.

Every Monday I go into downtown Austin to yoga class. On the way that Monday, I randomly opened Audible to listen to the end of Michael Singer's book, *The Surrender Experiment*.

His book is about recognizing that nobody knows how to care for you better than our Father. Our Father loves to grow His children. Michael teaches, if your happiness comes down to life or preference, life is going to win everytime. He means accepting your reality will position you to know reality, and to recognize the opportunities that are right under your nose. Through many decades of his life, he never said no to an opportunity to serve. He consciously set aside his preferences and agreed to challenges set before him. Michael wanted to quietly meditate in his temple in the Floridian woods, and yet God had other, grand plans for his innate talents.

I picked Michael's book back up on the way to yoga. I arrived at Monday night class with surrender on my heart. The first person I saw when I walked into class was none other than Sarah, the artist. She never came to that class. I did not know she was interested in yoga, nor did I know she went to that studio. Austin is a big city, after all.

We set up our mats adjacent and chatted a bit about life and about the painting. She was responding to my apparent reluctance when she said, "As soon as you're ready, we can use the down payment to go to the store to pick out a bunch of your favorite foods. We'll stage the thing. You are invited to come over once I get the staging pics for a feast..."

"Okay," I said.

She said, "Or if you would rather, you can just tell me your favorite foods and I will take care of it."

"Okay," I said again. Then class began.

When I got home later that night, I was going through the mail. In the mail was a check from my former home insurance company. Several months prior, when I first bought my house, I paid for an entire year of home insurance. The insurance company came out and looked at the house in the condition I bought it, and decided they did not want to cover me. The tree branches were too overgrown and in places were touching the rooftop. The deck was too high, plus it was rotting in places, there were no railings for safety purposes, and the crawlspace was wide open for a child to trap themselves...My house was, in its purchased condition, too much of a liability. When they called me to tell me their standards, they gave me 7 days to make a few thousand dollars of upgrades or they would cancel. I did not even attempt to save the policy. So, they canceled the policy and issued a refund check. They planned to acknowledge coverage while the policy was in effect, so I did not know if the refund check would be for $5 or $500.

I opened up the check. It was for $1220. Within $20 of the cost of the painting.

I deposited the check. When it cleared, I sent the down payment to Sarah.

In a span of four hours, I went from talking myself out of the painting to being re-commited to it. When I told one of my friends about the synchronicities, she responded with, "After all that, please tell me you got the painting..."

I told my friend, "At this point, I *can't not.*"

The way I see it, this was a contest between my head and my heart. Aside from my own clever rationalizations, such as the idea that this is an investment in a totem of gratitude, my head has a strong case against the fridge painting. All of the reasons not to buy the painting exist in my head. All of the desire and passion and excitement about the painting come from my heart. Electrically and magnetically the impressions my heart has on the universe are several hundred times stronger than those created by my head. Which means my head is largely fending for itself to get its way, while my heart is actively forming electromagnetic alliances.

The synchronicities are there. They have always been there, only my awareness and my willingness to listen needed time to catch up. Some of them are as heavy-handed as these. Some aren't. It will not always be as obvious as running into someone and getting a check for practically an exact amount. But they are there for you.

Just like you have a slightly different relationship with every one of your friends, so too does God have a unique relationship with you. If any of these synchronicities I received as guidance make you roll your eyes, understand that God is speaking to me in ways He thinks I can hear. The universe may work with you completely differently. But so long as you have a desire in your heart, God has designed a universe that contorts itself in response.

CHAPTER 3.6

intentionality

What the baseball, the yellow shovel, the blue bouncy ball, and the fridge painting represent are *intentions*. Whenever you are manifesting, you enter into a dance between intentionality and surrender. While you could run out to the store for any of these things, the point is to illustrate how to co-create, how to allow your intentions to run in the background of your life without any real effort to bring them about.

This is not to say you do nothing. This is to say that you are observant in identifying what to do. You set the intention, you begin to move, and you listen for guidance about where to move next.

Henry G. Bohn said, "The road to hell is paved with good intentions."

It has also been worded, "Hell is full of good meanings. Heaven is full of good works."

Manifesting does not need to take effort, but *action* is another story.

There is a difference between action and effort. Manifestation does not require effort, but it will require action - or *being*. If there is any effort involved, it is remembering that you are not the sole creator of your reality. You ask and you remain open to receive. You are a co-creator. Surrender is so vital because nothing needs to be forced. Efforting is a good indicator that you are not in a state of surrender. Surrendered or inspired action is different from *efforting*. Efforting feels like forcing something.

In the story about the baseball, when my dad and I were watching *The Patriot*, a sensation came over me to go for a sunset walk. I was stoked by the beauty of the golden light coming through the window. There was no effort involved, but there was inspired action. Intention and inspired action are a game-changing duo. It leads to an existence in a state of discovery.

If you are always relying on your own effort, there will come a time where you lack the energy to do anything. In America, we have a rise and grind culture that leaves a person emotionally, physically, and mentally fatigued. *You only have yourself,* they say. *Nobody is coming to save you.* The message is: "If it is to be, it's up to me."

In this culture, we are taught that we are in charge. The fate of the universe falls onto our shoulders, and none other. Nobody is coming. There is no savior. Pessimism arises out of this belief system, as we look around the world and disbelieve that any of us have the personal fortitude to overcome our sin nature. Or we look to a government party to save us. When we believe that we are in charge, and us alone, we tend to think of ourselves as separate. Physical might is so valued in this culture because forcing things is a natural part of a society where things must be accomplished through effort. *When a little effort does not do the trick, more effort must be necessary...*

A society that thinks like this leaves no room for surrender. This society gives little consideration to the inherent forces of nature. Seeing is believing. Nobody is coming. The resources are scarce and running out. I must get mine. I must compete. If it is to be, it is up to me. There are winners and there are losers.

If you ask a full-blooded member of this society to order the following list by importance, they would say:

- Physical
- Mental
- Emotional
- Spiritual

In some ways, I think of the Mandolorian, in the hit Star Wars spinoff series. If you watch the show, you find a man armed to the teeth with weaponry. He claims that weapons are his religion. He approaches an stone Jedi temple and when a long-distance connection is not made immediately, he searches for the communication controls. You cannot blame Mando for his naivety. When you live in a vast galaxy, everyone is naive. What you can see is real, and what you cannot see is less important. As Mando's character develops, the audience witnesses a slow reversal of these priorities.

the independent

A man intends to cross the desert. Rumor has it: gold and other precious things have been found on the other side. These rewards could be life changing for him. He fills his canteens with water, loads his packs with gear, and heads out. Nobody is going to stop him. He brings enough weapons to handily protect himself.

He is alone in the desolation. There are others about, but each individual is separate. Because they each only have what they can personally carry, there burgeons a dangerous atmosphere of competitiveness. Word spreads around what each person carries. The man with weapons side-eyes the man with shelter, thinks, "If I eliminate this man, I will sleep easier. I could do so, as he has nothing to protect himself with…"

And so he kills this man in the dead of night and takes his supplies. His pace slows with the weight of additional gear, but he is more secure. Eventually, this more comfortable and slow-moving man notices another man with water. The ambitious killer's weapons flash before the man-with-water ever has a chance to speak! He then steals his water and his other provisions and leaves him for dead. Now the man-with-weapons has shelter, water, and safety. This man is weighed down heavily by his cargo, but he carries on. That night, the well-provisioned looter hears another man traveling in the night. He hears the sound of camels. He thinks, *This is my opportunity to save myself.* He does what has become normal - he kills. In the commotion, one camel is injured while the others become startled and run off into the desert. In the pursuit of a camel, the man becomes exhausted. He perishes. His body is soon covered in sand, and his weapons, his water, and his tent are covered with it.

✦　✦　✦

This man set out with the intention of crossing the desert alone. This man forced his way forward with fear. This man ran out of energy and perished.

When you appreciate the lengths God will go to co-create with you, you begin to laugh at the futility of *forcing things*. It is great news to realize that you have been over-exerting yourself. Everything is so much easier than you have been making it. In other words, I have good news and I have bad news. The good news is everything your heart desires is within your grasp. The bad news is that it has always been, but you have been trying too hard. A great paradox of life is that our effort to fight in order to receive something in one way often blocks it from coming to us in another. The act of fighting attaches us to the means to an end, we become identified with our tactics, and in doing so, we become blind to other ways.

When you get crystal clear on your intention, and even go so far as to understand how this intention connects with your deep desires, opportunity knocks.

the hazy intention

However, surface level intentions are like shining objects to a raccoon. In the pursuit of one, you might be distracted by another.

A man intends to cross the desert. Rumor has it: gold and other precious things have been found on the other side. These rewards could be life changing for him. He fills his canteens with water, loads his packs with gear, and...

He overhears a handful of travelers talking about a ship that sank carrying precious cargo in the sea nearby. These rewards could be life changing for him. He takes a sip of water and contemplates his options. Now a man intends to retrieve the sunken treasure.

While provisioning himself for his new quest, he comes across a man leading four camels. The man politely asks him, "Will you be needing a camel for your venture, good sir? I have three I must deliver across the desert, but buy any one of your choosing!"

"You sell camels?" the man asks.

"Buy, sell, trade, rescue. It is honest business," the man says.

The man contemplates this new information. He asks the camel seller a few additional questions with intrigue. By the end of the conversation, a man intends to enter into the camel business.

✦ ✦ ✦

intentions rising

At times, it can seem like there are a thousand roads to your destination, and yet you cannot choose one. None of them are quite right, so somehow all of them are quite wrong. You rest your head at night on comfortable intentions. Dreams become like pillows. You think that *someday* you will wake up and it will be real. Time trickles by steadily. Eventually you have packed your pillow so full of dreams that it is lumpy and uncomfortable. Now all of your unfulfilled dreams keep you up at night.

Becoming crystal clear on your intention is a process. One of my mentors coaches taking yourself through a series of "*I want that because...*" exercises.

A man intends to cross the desert. Rumor has it: gold and other precious things have been found on the other side. These rewards could be life changing for him. He fills his canteens with water, loads his packs with gear, and heads out. He brings enough weapons to handily protect himself. Nobody is going to stop him.

"That's a lotta knives," a man standing by a well says to him.

"Heading across the desert," he explains.

The man-at-the-well nods. "Why's that? 'Cuz of the gold rush?" he guesses.

"That's right."

"What you gonna do wit the gold?"

"It's gonna be mine," the man says simply. W "I am gonna have it. I will be rich. That's what."

"You want the gold so you'll be rich..." the man-at-the-well repeats. "Why do you want to be rich?"

The man thinks that's a stupid question, but he can plainly see this man will not be of any harm to him. He seems a simpleton, with simple-minded questions. He decides to indulge him with a thoughtful answer. "I want to be rich because rich folks got no worries."

"I see," the man-at-the-well responds. "So you crossing the desert to eliminate your worries. Why do you hate worries so much?"

The man should have seen that simple follow-up question coming. Again he decides to indulge the man with conversation. "I have been worried my whole life. I am at the end of my rope," he answers. "Once I get these worries outta the way, I am going to settle down somewhere and raise some kits." The man took on a wistful look as he imagined the days he has always dreamed about - days with wealth, with a wife, with children, with land, with animals.

"I see," the man-at-the-well says. "You crossin' the desert for a family."

The man thinks that's a simple remark, but agrees nonetheless. "S'pose I am."

"Why you want that?"

"A family?" the man asks. "Well, ain't nothing more important than family."

The man-at-the-well smiles. "My sister always says the same thing, mister. Take care on your quest."

Now our protagonist has a lot more clarity about what he is truly after. It is not about gold, or gemstones, or sunken treasure, or camels. It is about family. It is about taking those swirling dreams out of dreamland and making them real. Now he can be freed from the confusion that arises out of his lack of clarity, and listen for the opportunities to satisfy what his heart truly desires. Now he can get out of his own way when God is trying to co-create with him. Understand, this entire time God has known the contents of his heart, but the man's truth has been veiled by thinking it all was completely up to him.

Asking yourself *"why do I want that?"* repeatedly may not change your actions, but it will change your heart about those actions. Suddenly, this man is not crossing the desert with weapons to hoard gold and riches, but is keeping his heart on a swivel for what he deeply desires.

Your heart does not deeply desire *stuff*. The language of your heart is emotion. Your heart desires to be open, and as a result of its openness, fulfilled. Deep down or perhaps just below the surface, you are aware of the futility of feeding your heart stuff. Stuff does not fulfill. *Meaning fulfills.*

Don Draper, my favorite TV ad man, says in the show Mad Men, "But what is happiness? It's the moment before you need more happiness." Stuff is a single letter of the language of your heart. You cannot articulate what the heart longs to say with *stuff*.

You may intend to go get something, but take the time to understand what emotion you are searching for. Go deep. If it is an emotion you desire, like love and fulfillment, then by doing this exercise you will free yourself from attachment to any particular *stuff*. You will identify what you are really after.

surrendered intention

A man intends to cross the desert. Rumor has it: gold and other precious things have been found on the other side. These rewards could be life changing for him. He fills his canteens with water, loads his packs with gear, and heads out. He brings enough weapons to handily protect himself. Nobody is going to stop him.

He is alone in the desolation. There are others about, but each individual is separate. Because they each only have what they can personally carry, there burgeons a dangerous atmosphere of competitiveness. Word spreads around what each person carries. The man with weapons side-eyes the man with shelter, thinks, "This man is in danger of being robbed. I know because the heinous thought crossed my own mind. Perhaps my protection will be worth sharing his shelter."

A quick, tense discussion creates an alliance between the men. There was something between them that enabled trust, and it became formed. They traveled the next day with much more comfort than either thought possible.

Until a hearty thirst begins to press them into the hot sand. Walking is grueling. Even setting up the tents exhausts them.

That night, at camp, a third man lumbers by well after dark. By the shape of his hunched-over silhouette, both men can see that he, too, is worse for wear. "My man," they call out to him. "Can we offer a fellow wearied traveler a suitable place to rest? There is an empty corner within this shelter that may do you well."

The pained man rejects their proposal, "A trick," he says, carrying on.

They do not try to stop him. They watch him go. A few minutes later, they watch the man collapse into a heap of tired bones. Both of them muster what strength they have, retrieve the man, and lay his weak body down to rest in the corner of the shelter.

In the morning, he wakes with surprise. "You brought me in?" he says. He checks himself to find everything intact, "You did not rob me?" he says.

"We did you no great favor," the armed man says. "We each chose wrongly what to carry across the desert. I chose steel, but steel offers no protection from the blistering sun. My companion chose shelter, but shelter is heavy and burdensome to carry. What water we brought is gone, and our will to carry on has gone with it."

"No man is a failure who has friends," the man-with-shelter announces. "At least we will not perish as failures."

"I, too, chose poorly," the rescued man says. "I have only now found what I should have brought from town. It is as you said: friends. Because, *friends*, in my packs here, I carry an oppressive quantity of water."

A celebratory wonderment passes through the tent. The man-with-water shares, and throughout the next day, the three of them sit in their tents resting and recovering. They hydrate themselves out of the sight of the searing sun. They are contemplating taking a second day of rest when they hear a commotion outside.

It is the sound of a man protecting his camels from ambush. The three men arm themselves from the first's armory, and leap to his aid. A skirmish unfolds, but the help of the three succeed in protecting the old man and his four camels.

With the bandits scared off, the four men take stock of each other. "Would you like some water?" one asks the old man. "Here, come inside out of the sun." The old man does as they suggest, all the while staring at them with a disoriented expression - as though he was sure he was hallucinating.

"I saw you three in town," he says eventually. "You are prospectors."

They nod.

He says, "I would offer you each a camel to ride, but I only have one to spare."

"That's a nice thought," one of the prospectors said. "Riding would be a welcome change. If only we were on our way back, then we would have the gold to buy him."

"Well, my life is certainly worth this camel," the old man says. "I owe you that much." The old man peels a set of reins from this bundle and hands them to a prospector.

"That's mighty generous, sir," the man-with-shelter says. "S'pose we can each take turns riding."

The armed man imagines crossing the desert on foot in his condition. He is worn out. Two men might survive sharing one camel, but not three. An idea strikes him. He says, "Those bandits are going to circle back. Will you accept an escort home, sir? I can offer my protection on the way. Perhaps this service will be worth something to you."

The old man readily accepts.

The next morning, two men travel west with a camel to share, and the other two men ride north.

When the old man and the armed man arrive in the village, they are greeted by a beautiful trio. The old man introduces them, "This is my wife, my son and my daughter," he says.

The young man gets down off his camel to meet them. He cannot pull his eyes off of the man's daughter, for she is like an oasis of splendor...

✦   ✦   ✦

You cannot surrender and maintain your separation.

God will use you for the fulfillment of others as often as He uses others for your fulfillment. This fusion of utility forms one machine that functions for the good of all. Effectively there are no others.

Our determination to remain separate only cuts us off from the flow. The first two letters of God spell "go". Love is a verb. Intentions are fine and dandy, but they mean nothing if they are not conjoined with action. Albeit, all action is not created equal. Surrendered action is key. Surrendered action can only be recognized in the present. Surrendered action maintains the awareness that you are not separate from the system, but a living-breathing part of it.

Surrendered action is like sailing. You pull too hard on the sail - that is, you use force - your boat will tip over. You do not pull hard enough - that is, you set no intentions and take no action - your boat will list lifelessly, going wherever you are blown. A sailboat can travel against the wind, but it does so by sinking a deep, grounded rudder. It holds onto God. Surrendered action keeps you in the world without making you part of it. The wind and the current do not dictate your direction, your intentions and your connection with God do. Without the manipulation of the sail - your intentions - and without the depth of the rudder - God - a sailboat is just a piece of driftwood.

Surrendered action is also like archery. The archer is one with her bow, always. Her energy is the bowstring. The archer must always mind the condition of her bow. It cannot always be engaged energetically. She must take off the string. She must let her bow rest. This will allow the bow to respond properly to the tensions involved in inspired action.

Her arrows are her intentions. An archer sets an intention with the direction of the arrow. The target is justified by the archers' intentions. It is set aside when it is selected. It may be a long way off.

When shooting, the archer assumes elegant posture. She engages with the aligned energy, looks down her intentions to her target, and uses her intuition to time the shot with the winds of the universe. In this way, shooting unites the archer and the universe.

When the arrow is released, there is nothing left to do but watch and learn.

The archers body will turn and face the target, watching from an open-hearted position of vulnerability. Set your intentions. Align with the universe. Let loose your arrows. Watch and learn. The way of the bow is the way of joy and enthusiasm, of perfection and error, of technique and instinct.

This is the way of surrendered action.

This is the way of the *Detourist*.

- Spiritual
- Emotional
- Mental
- Physical

Once aligned with the nurturing forces of the universe, you give the charge to a higher power. You can become reliant on Him, and not on your own physical and mental effort.

e for effort

Just like there is a difference between force and *power*, making and *creating*, let's discuss the differences between effort and *action*.

Please know that throughout this section, I am taking liberties with language in an attempt at exactness. I do not wish to turn anyone into the Effort Police. I am using these words because they illustrate my point, but also because I have a personal affinity with them. If effort has always been something you have associated with hard work and going the extra mile, I might lose you here. Feel free to substitute effort whenever necessary with words like: force, fight, compulsion, coercion, pressure, or rigidity.

How can we differentiate *surrendered* action and *compulsive effort?*

One day I was out front of my house building a wine cabinet for a customer. I was shaving off hundreds of little pieces of wood, and suddenly a memory popped into my head:

My grandfather was standing at the back of his Suburban on our annual family camping trip. He had brought all the firewood we would need from his personal supply, and he was instructing my cousins and me to lug the logs next to the firepit. One by one we went, until I had a bright idea. I brought over a tarp, I set it on the ground, we loaded all of the wood onto it quickly, and then we dragged the thing in one fell swoop over to the fire pit. *Job done.*

Grandpa said, "If you want a job done efficiently, hire a lazy man to do it."

One of us said, "Who's lazy? You didn't carry a single log, grandpa."

In the present, building the wine cabinet, I was wishing for a tarp for all of these wood shards and shavings. After I was finished cleaning up, I was regretting the inefficiency of having to take armfuls to my backyard trip after trip. I considered tossing the pieces over my fence into the backyard where they would be out of place but still *"put away"*.

Not fifteen minutes later, a giant gust of wind shook my trees. And a tarp blew across my front yard.

When the project was finished, I loaded all of the pieces onto the tarp and dragged it out back. That's an A for surrendered action.

I have efforted my way through life more times than I care to count. Effort does not always leave you empty-handed, but it does leave you empty-tanked. What spoils arrive through effort are limited by your stubborn endurance. Eventually you will find the end of your rope, and effort can last no more.

For five years I sold cancer insurance. The sales pitch for cancer insurance sounds a lot like a mob boss trying to threaten a mark. "You love ya family? It'd be a cryin' shame if sometin' happen to 'em."

There are two ways to influence people. You can show them heaven or you can show them hell.

Showing heaven is guiding someone's focus to their hopes and dreams. It is helping people see a path to a future they feel called to. You show them that they have angels, that they are protected, and they can give a great gift to God by using their God-given gifts. You encourage their inner-creative-child out to envisage the world more like a playground.

Showing hell is painting a vision of a future that nobody wants to give any energy to. It is using pointed questions, statistics, and fearmongering to reveal the customer's needs. In many cases, if the questions are clever enough, *revealing* a need is indistinguishable from *manufacturing* a need. Once you have the need hovering between you and the prospect, you can offer a solution. What you offer is not the best solution, but a solution that can immediately remedy the anxiety your questions have just raised. While there is no impetus within the transaction toward a higher ideal, in the end you will go home feeling like you have done a good service for your followers, and your followers will thank you if they ever have to use your product. We all sing kumbaya because we are *of the world* together.

I have no regrets about selling cancer insurance. That career path helped me get to the end of my rope in a hurry. The role was five years of effort, and it emptied my tank in a hurry. That was an E for effort.

reflection

Take a minute to consider your own life. *What are you forcing into place?* As long as we stay out of alignment, we block what is in alignment. Do you get the Sunday Scaries - the dread associated with going to work tomorrow?

Inspect your relationship, your friendships, your profession, the standard operating procedures within your life, the expectations that you feel pressing you into a particular shape.

> IF YOU TRULY WANT TO GIVE THOUGHT AND CONSIDERATION TO WHERE YOU ARE OUT OF ALIGNMENT, WHERE YOU ARE EXHAUSTING YOURSELF WITH EFFORT, AND COME UP WITH CLARITY ON HOW TO MOVE FORWARD, DOWNLOAD A FREE COPY OF THE COLLIDE-O-SCOPE. GO TO WWW.MATTHEWEMMOREY.COM/COLLIDEOSCOPE.

Please free yourself from one area of effort. Stop forcing that one thing, and watch how much energy you regain for yourself.

If there is a friendship that always leaves you feeling drained, it is okay to see that person less. Friendship ought to be effortless. My best friendships are defined by kindness, compassion, laughter, and inspired action. When I told my Denver-based friend Alex that I was looking for positions in Colorado, he loaned me his car, took me around the city to his favorite places, helped me envision my future, ate donuts and drank coffee with me, cracked jokes, and made it a hilarious day for the both of us. When I was working in insurance, he encouraged me to do something creative. When I was recovering from a break-up, he took a two thousand mile road trip with me across three national parks. As Bob Goff says, "Love does." Alex exemplifies inspired, surrendered action. Our friendship is expectation-less. Our friendship is effortless. Yet Alex's example proves it is not action-less.

Only you can know what you are forcing into place. As I mentioned in a previous chapter, our safety-oriented minds crave definition. It is not uncommon to hastily define something while it ought to remain in discovery.

I was often heard in my insurance days saying, "This is the last career I will ever have." That felt really good to say. I did not know at the time that this line was perpetuating misalignment. When I was fired, it was the best thing that could have happened for me. I was forced back into discovery.

Recalculating your life to be effortless is not without its complications. The location of your misalignment is there to be felt, waiting to be understood, asking to be adjusted. Our culture simultaneously celebrates effort while telling us things should be effortless. Surrendered, inspired action *is* effortless, though.

Bottomline: If you have to abandon a part of yourself to make something fit, you are forcing it. If a conversation cannot or has not remedied the issue, the most surrendered action is to undefine the defined, and move back into a state of discovery. Find what fits effortlessly.

the love list

Ready for another gratitude practice?

Beauty is in the eye of the beholder. When I hear the leaves on a birch tree clapping in the wind, I am teleported back to Ludington, Michigan where my family holds our annual camping trip. A clip show of photographs and memories shutter through my mind, and invariably, I feel good.

Over the last ten years, when I see something random and obscure that elicits that internal warmth, I add it to my Love's List. It has slowly grown into what it is today. When I am feeling down, I simply remember my favorite things and then I don't feel so bad...

HERE IS MY LIST THUS FAR

MORNING "MOUNTAIN CLOUDS"

FARMERS MARKETS

LEAVES THAT CLAP IN THE WIND

COUNTRY TRAINS ROLLING SILENTLY IN THE DISTANCE

ABANDONED MINES

BREAKFAST WITH FAMILY

SPLIT RAIL FENCES

THE FEEL OF GRASS UNDERFOOT

SITTING COMFORTABLY UNDER LAMPLIGHT

CRACKING BONFIRES

THE SCRATCHY STATIC OF VINYL RECORD PLAYERS

WARMING MY HANDS WITH HOT COFFEE

RAIN ON A TIN ROOF

THE AUTUMN NIP IN THE AIR

DISTANT DRUMS / MUSIC

SHADE BENEATH GREAT TREES

SAWDUST

OLD BARNS

COLD CLEAR MORNINGS

SWIRLING STEAM ON A COLD DAY

EXPOSED BRICK INTERIOR

THE BONFIRE SMELL

EXPOSED PIPE FITTINGS

WICKER LAMPSHADES

MAPLE SYRUP

SMELL OF SNOW AND ICE

SMELL OF DECAYING LEAVES

SLIDING MY FEET ON WOODEN FLOORBOARDS

ITALIAN RESTAURANT CURTAINS

ARCADES

SMELL OF CHLORINE

BEING SCARED IN THE WOODS

COUNTRY POWER LINE LAMPS

RUNNING FULL SPEED

BEACH GRASS

FOOTBALL RADIO BROADCASTS

SKIPPING STONES

TELLING STORIES WITH FRIENDS

SOLO ADVENTURES

GAME NIGHTS WITH FRIENDS

UNEXPLAINABLE HAPPINESS

A COLLECTION OF MATCHBOOKS

SOUNDS OF A COFFEE MAKER

GIANT ORNATE WELCOME ARCHWAYS

LYING ON WARM CONCRETE

FEELING IN SHAPE AND FLEXIBLE

AN OPEN ROAD

LIVE MUSIC

GIANT PINE TREES

OLD GYMNASIUMS AND ARMORIES

BUILDINGS BUILT INTO HILLS

FARM ANIMALS

STONE LABYRINTHS

MAKING CORNY SONGS

GHOST HUNTS

COLLECTING SEA-GLASS

GOING OFF-ROADING

PINE NEEDLES UNDER TALL PINES

DAYDREAMING

GRASSY KNOLLS WITH A VIEW

THINGS LOST BEHIND DRAWERS

MOUNTAINSIDE VILLAGES

ROAD TRIP PIT STOPS

BEVERAGES

MOTOR INNS

THE MIST OVER WATERFALLS

A NEON OASIS

SITTING IN NOSTALGIA

POWERFUL ENGINE SOUNDS

A HOT MUG ON A COLD DAY

TIME WITH FAMILY

FEELING THE RHYTHM

CENTURY OLD ARCHITECTURE

DRIVES THROUGH SMALL TOWNS

SMALL TOWN DINERS

THE TRUTH

BEING SNEAKY

FRIENDSHIPS THAT DON'T LOSE A BEAT

DAYS IN BED AND THE LINE: "COME BACK TO BED"

EFFORTLESS INTIMACY AND UNDERSTANDING

QUIET TIME WITH GOD

CELEBRATING WITH PEOPLE

COMING ALONG FOR CHORES

SIMPLE GESTURES OF LOVE

SUNLIGHT FILTERING THROUGH TREES

SUNBEAMS

LEARNING NEW CONSTELLATIONS

DUNES

COLD WATER PLUNGES

SCALING BOULDERS

CHOPPING WOOD

WOODWORKING

FOSSIL HUNTING

HOT SHOWERS AFTER COLD SWIMS

NURSERIES

THE SUN MAKING PLANTS GLOW GREEN

MADE UP GAMES

FALL FLAVORS

COOL DRAFTS AND WARM COFFEE

BUILDING DAMS

DUSTY FEET

HAMMOCKS OVER CREEKS

HEARTY SANDWICHES

CLIMBING TREES

ROCK BRIDGES

DOG TOYS IN NEW PLACES

DOGS CHOWING DOWN IN THE MIDDLE OF THE NIGHT

CEDAR

WOOLY SOCKS

STACKS OF FIREWOOD

BRIGHT COLORS

MEAT FREEZERS

BIRDS AT THE FEEDER

Beauty is in the eye of the beholder because we do not see with our eyes, we see with our minds. When I watch a bird at the feeder, you might see a finch, but I see my grandmother.

I added this last one to the list in October 2021. In late October, I got a strong urge to hang bird feeders around my property. I bought three and hung them in the trees outside my office window. When I told my sister about the chore, she pointed out that our grandma had passed away exactly two years prior, and oh, *how she loved to watch birds*. She knew all their names and their favorite seeds. Bird watching was a love that she had demonstrated for all my siblings and cousins in our youth. The bird feeders and all the birds that would visit seemed her way of creating an activity for us to enjoy together. Now everyday I get some time with grandma.

These are portals to love. In the great Collide-o-scope, these are the warm colored crystals.

Now begin your own list. Look around you at the things that spark joy in your present. Store the list somewhere so when you experience some unexpected bliss, you can add its source to the list. Watch it grow. Slowly, you are training your mind to look for small blessings. Eventually, we all will see them everywhere.

the grimace

The goal of working through the *Collide-o-scope* is to conditional yourself with positivity.

There is always a variety of things to look at in your field of vision. Each of these things carries a particular energy for you, the beholder. Things are meaningful for you because of the meaning you give them. Because life imitates art more than art imitates life, we must be mindful of our environment.

Environment is a dynamic term. It refers to your intellectual and nutritional diet, your beliefs, your relationships, your surroundings, and in general, the meaning you ascribe to the things around you.

When you are out for a run, the moment you get tired, a dark beckoning crystal presents itself. This dark crystal is your discomfort. If you focus on it, it gets bigger. The crystals you make into your focal point fractal off and multiply, just as they do with a kaleidoscope. On a long run, emphasizing your discomfort by focusing on it will likely bring your run to a hasty end.

When Hercules fights the hydra, he finds cutting off its head causes two more heads to grow in its place. Focusing on discomfort is a lot like fighting a hydra. It will grow until it fills your entire field of vision. You will be much more equipped to overcome its cause if you are not simultaneously multiplying it.

We are stronger than we think.

We are capable of taking much more in stride that we know.

We just ought not focus on our pain.

I love Wim Hof's encouragement in his breathwork sessions. He says, *"Allow your body to do what your body is capable of doing."*

While running a half marathon with my mom in 2019, we were aiming to finish in under two hours. She never had. We fell into stride with the 1:55 pace setter, but around the ten mile mark, we lost sight of it. At the eleven mile mark, my mom's stride twisted. She bit her lip, her head was cocked off to one side, she grimaced, and people slowly but steadily began passing us. A lifetime of running coaches rose up inside my head, and I passed along their coaching: "Mom, straighten up your stride. Breath! Face strong. Smile. We got this!" She straightened up, she held her expression strong, she focused on her breathing, and we crossed the finish line with a time of 1:59:47.

When her focus was on her discomfort, her grimace rippled through her entire posture. Her running form mutated into something hard and inefficient. For the last two miles, she stopped multiplying dark crystals by focusing on her breath, her form, and her posture. Instead of her *Collide-o-scope* becoming overrun by awareness of discomfort, she focused on her controllables: mindset, form, breath, expression.

People talk about this when they do ice plunges. The desire is to clench, to try to muscle through the discomfort. This is just another way of focusing on your discomfort. You cannot fight cold, you can only embrace it. You relax, you breathe through it. Your emotional state takes cues from your body language. Your body language is a reflection of your mind, your mental state. When your posture reflects *pain*, you are mentally focused on your pain, and your experience is pain. When your bodily and facial posture reflect poise, your mental state is strong, and your whole experience changes.

This is because your mind informs your brain which in turn controls your body. Your mind is your *Collide-o-scope*, your internal disposition, a collection of your focuses. If your body is contorted in discomfort, that discomfort is housed in your mind. If your body is held in poise, the discomfort shifts into the background in favor of more optimum focuses. Anesthesia; multiple personalities with different physiologies; allergies; facial structures; and the fact that some people *"catch"* colds while others do not are all evidence that your experience begins in the mind. Where the mind is asleep there is no experience, and where the mind is identified the experience differs.

To me, my breath and my posture are the blue crystals. The calming, peaceful, baptismal waters.

I first had this revelation when getting a deep tissue massage. I found I had two completely different experiences based on how I dealt with the pain. If I recoiled, clenched and grimaced, I tended to hold my breath, and the pain became quite unbearable. I would leave the massage therapist without getting the results I went in for.

When I literally pressed my breath into the area the therapist was working on, I experienced a deep catharsis. My exhales became timed with her deepest work, and instead of experiencing unbearable pain, I experienced emotive release. My focus was on my face and my breath. I would not grimace. If I grimaced, my mind had begun to believe the discomfort was unbearable, the evidence of which appeared in my facial posture. *"This is not going to kill you, Matthew. This is going to help you,"* I said to myself. Somehow, knowing that I was not going to die lessened the drama I was reflecting onto the situation. With my mind settled, my face relaxed, and my breath intentionally guided, I had barely any focus leftover for my pain.

James Redfield says, "Where attention goes, energy flows. Where intention goes, energy flows!"

Eileen Wilder, a friend and fellow author, shared some of her mentor's favorite words with me: "I give no energy to unfavorable outcomes." Which basically means, do not put any attention on what you do not want to multiply.

Remember your *Collide-o-scope*.

At any moment, you can look at any crystal you choose. You can focus on problems or you can focus on solutions, which often is a way of being that eradicates the problem without identifying with it. You can focus on pain or you can focus on your posture. You can focus on your fears or you can focus on your dreams.

MATTHEW 6:23-24 READS,

"The eye is the lamp of the body. If your eyes are healthy, your whole body will be full of light. But if your eyes are unhealthy, your whole body will be full of darkness. If then the light within you is darkness, how great is that darkness! No one can serve two masters. Either you will hate the one and love the other, or you will be devoted to the one and despise the other. You cannot serve both God and money."

If your eyes are healthy, focused on goodness, your whole body will be full of light. Put your eyes on warm-colored crystals - like loving solutions, like God, like play, like your simple pleasures. In the midst of pain, put your eyes on your peace, your breath, your Strength, and on the good Word, through prayer and scripture. Go for hikes, eat colorful foods, propagate plants for your house, look around! And remember the most essential truth of the Collide-o-scope: *What you appreciate appreciates.*

By doing this you will plant in your field of vision a gallery of beauty.

CHAPTER 4

unconscious competence

The narrower our field of vision, the more likely we are to put ourselves at the center of the story. The more expansive our field of vision, the closer we get to being able to see things through God's knowing eyes.

After a break-up, my therapist said, "Look, if you are not God's best match for her, then she is not God's best match for you." That one line helped me to stop thinking that I had blown my chance to get the thing that would make me happiest. "What is meant for you will never pass you by," is another helpful one.

Sewn within both of these helpful lines is *trust*. Trust is knowing that as time goes on, as you get closer to alignment, life will improve. You were created to be very good, to be in the flow of abundance, for a good purpose. The more you operate out of Self, the more *"best matches"* you are going to find, and the less alarmed you will be about things passing you by.

The relationship did not work out?

You did not get the job?

Something you were excited about fell through?

Take the lesson and keep on living in alignment.

My therapist also says, "God never takes anything away without replacing it with something better." We were talking about jobs and relationships at the time, not the deaths of loved ones. But we can even look at these painful losses from God's knowing. After reading Chris Lippincott's book *Spirits Beside Us*, I have come to know that what my deceased loved ones have gained is far more than I have lost. And in actuality, these people are not as lost as I once thought.

expanding the collide-o-scope

I have constructed a list of *small shifts* that powerfully expand our Collide-o-scopes. Being intentional in these areas will gradually add *trust* to your worldview. There are thousands of uses for expanded awareness.

1. **Take care of your gut.** Drink pre and probiotics. Balance your pH. Your microbiome is a sophisticated neural network that transmits messages from trillions of bacteria. The brain in your gut exerts a powerful influence over the one in your head. Gut bacteria produce hundreds of neurochemicals that the brain uses to regulate basic physiological processes as well as mental processes such as learning, memory, and mood. For example, gut bacteria manufacture about 95 percent of the body's supply of serotonin, which influences both mood and gastrointestinal activity.

2. **Chew more.** It takes energy for your body to digest your food. Chewing more will create less energy losses, increase gratitude,

and change your facial structure. The increase in chewing will strengthen your face, expand your nasal passages and aid nose-breathing. You should breathe through your nose as much as possible. Chewing more, as our ancestors did, will create ripples of positivity through your anatomy.

3. **Hydrate.** Hydrogen and oxygen are essential elements in fuels. Water is two parts hydrogen and one part oxygen. When you are hydrating, you are giving yourself battery life. Essentially all of your bodily functions require water to carry them out properly. Alkaline water is a good option to satisfy Shift #1, as well.

4. **Have Quiet Time.** Care for your soul. Take time to journal, write letters, take a bath, take a walk, sit still. I like to think of my thoughts as a plinko board. At the top are my compulsive thoughts, the ones that drop in out of nowhere. At the bottom are the thoughts I rarely have, because all of the louder, compulsive ones have already gotten my attention. Sometimes, at the bottom, minutes can go by without a thought. *Ahhh.* Plus, meditation is better than sitting around doing nothing...

5. **Have The Hard Conversation whenever possible.** Seek resolution with people. Not necessarily reconciliation, but resolution. The bad blood between you and another is bad blood inside you. Avoiding conflict is a close cousin to self abandonment. Understanding another person's perspective will unlock never-before-seen crystals in the kaleidoscope.

6. **Be charitable.** Support just causes.

7. **Enthuse your inner child.** Meaning, try new things with a spirit of play. No need to identify with your baseline abilities. If you

like it, you can train and get better. If you don't like it, then you get a bonus point for knowing for sure.

8. **Tell people you love them.** I challenge you to tell 15 people, whom you don't ordinarily tell, that you love them. Maybe you think you are "not that type of person". The more nervous resistance you feel to this idea, the more completing the challenge will set you free. You can text them!

9. **Use a person's name.** We live in a pretty transactional world. People are dehumanized. Using a person's name lets them know that you see them and care about them. As we discussed in the chapter on clarity, a person's name carries a vibration that they will meet with warm affinity. Want to make a new friend? Naturally use their name around them.

10. **Spend time in nature.**

11. **Always be gentle with yourself.** It is said that self love is merely accepting the grace that you have been adamantly denying yourself. God Willing, life is long enough to observe where you can improve without evaluating yourself and identifying with your failures.

12. **Go barefoot.** *Earthing* is the process of grounding yourself to the Earth's healing electricity. You can walk around barefoot, have an indoor earthing mat, or some athletes sleep using electrically conductive devices. Earthing reduces inflammation, pain, and stress; improves blood flow, sleep, and vitality. We discussed the science of Earthing in chapter 2.

13. **Sit down for dinner.** Spend the time to pray, eat, appreciate, talk, break bread with friends and family, and form your community.

14. **Keep your word.** Speak the truest truth. Say what you mean and mean what you say. Feel free to talk things through with people in the moment. "I am feeling a little resistance to that idea" is a fine way to feel more deeply into something when part of you wants to say no. *Or just no.* Jesus told us not to swear by anything. Our no, or our yes, is enough.

15. **Travel.**

16. **Take lots of book recommendations.**

17. **Take a genuine interest in people.**

18. **Get to know Christ for yourself.** Jesus was harsh toward the overly religious folks of His time. In His time, many religious people were elitist, judgemental, exclusionary, hypocritical, and condemning. He called them a *brood of vipers* for their maliciousness, and *white-washed tombs*, for how they made themselves shiny on the outside while being dead on the inside. He sought out the very people who feel unwelcome in church nowadays, and loved them. He is worth knowing, and seeking a relationship with.

These small shifts, when implemented, will create an overflow of trust in your life.

IF YOU HAVE NOT DOWNLOADED YOUR FREE COPY OF COLLIDE-O-SCOPE YET, DO SO NOW AT WWW.MATTHEWEMMOREY.COM/COLLIDEOSCOPE

using the collide-o-scope

With this newfound trust, you might be inclined to believe that you are supposed to go after your dream life. There are so many things that have been circling you since forever. You have dreams. You have ideals. The following list is to invigorate your creativity. This list is about making them real.

1. **Ask specifically for what you want / need.** Be clear about what is important to you, and be clear about asking for it.

2. **Use your creation energy wisely.** Don't be leaky with your creation energy. Be engaged within your creation. Be passionate. Be present. Creation energy is sexual energy, it is your imagination, it is you in the act of creating, it is time with God. Be mindful.

3. **Exercise.** I recommend yoga. Yoga is one of my favorites. Exercise is actually just a side effect of yoga. The true purpose of yoga is to be one with your breath and the present moment.

4. **Mix in a burst of cold shower.** This practice has too many health benefits to name. Not to mention, the psychological benefit of reframing your relationship with discomfort. Your dreams are going to require you to step out of your comfort zone. You might as well get used to thriving in discomfort.

5. **Have a morning routine.** What it consists of is less important than its existence. Find the routine that works for you.

6. **Write down your intentions.** And then spend time with them. Deliberately condition yourself in the direction of your dream.

7. **Prioritize.** In every season of life, identify what is most important to you. Make a list and organize it. That way in a moment of decision, you will have a guidepost to direct you. I choose: Scripture before phone. Water before coffee. Rocks before pebbles. Rocks are the important things I do not want to live without, like family. Pebbles are great but they aren't imperative, like going out drinking with friends. Sand is even less important stuff, like television.

8. **Create margin.** Allow yourself enough time to *be*. Practice the ruthless elimination of hurry. You will do more harm than good with an attitude of frustration.

9. **Take pride in your work.**

10. **Make compounding commitments.** A compounding commitment is one which amplifies your ability to commit to things in other areas of your life. For example, when I was vegetarian for a year, I found smaller commitments came easier because they were in the shadow of a big commitment. When I exercised every morning, I saw positive ripples in what I ate for breakfast, how much energy I had, and how I used that energy to get further ahead.

11. Pray. Have a conversation with God. Talk things through. Get to know His voice. It may sound a lot like yours. Jesus talks inside me as my highest intuition. You cannot pray wrong. Talk to God as you would a close friend.

These small shifts, when implemented, will create a unification of direction in your life.

With this unified direction, everything will be easier. You will hear your name being called, and you will be ready to answer. It will feel good to answer. You have laid all the groundwork and built the structure, all you have left to do is *say yes* when the opportunities arise.

maintaining the collide-o-scope

I have created one final list.

This list is about setting yourself up for success. Life is always happening, and with it, countless opportunities to subtly fall out of alignment. This final list is your checks and balances. Doing these things will help you use the Collide-o-scope to see life through God's knowing eyes.

1. **Have a standing appointment with your therapist.** Standing means routine, scheduled, and non-negotiable.

2. **Wake up at least 90 minutes before work.** Give yourself adequate time for your morning routine and for moving slowly. Your wake-up time is an extension of your bedtime, so mind them both properly.

3. **Get enough sleep.**

4. **Buy an alarm clock.** And put it on the other side of the room. Force yourself to get up. If your alarm clock is your phone, then you will be tempted to look at all your unread emails, texts, social media notifications...You could be thinking about whatever random headline you see fifteen seconds into your morning. Catholics have a term: liturgy. It is the form or formation of mass. It is how we worship. Our days become like liturgies, where we worship what we prioritize. Are you using your phone as a tool, or are you worshiping it?

5. **Keep a daily journal.** Have a minimum amount of time or pages that you will fill. Really work things out. Make it part of your morning routine.

6. **Set boundaries.** Your boundaries are your responsibility. If someone crosses your boundary and you say nothing, there is no boundary. Do not expect others to uphold your boundaries for you.

7. **Go without.** Practice sensory deprivation. Yogis call is *pratyahara*. Make pratyahara a common practice. When you feel yourself *wanting* something, make a practice out of withholding gratification. Self control, delayed gratification, and sensory deprivation are simple ways to overcome our compulsory thoughts. Don't buy the gum at the register just because it's there. Blindfold yourself for an evening and go without one of your primary senses. Leave your phone behind when you go for an outing.

8. **Don't make assumptions.** Our minds are story-tellers. We are inclined to jump to conclusions when we feel we have all the details of the story. We rarely do. If you are prone to making assumptions, keep a mental tally of all the times your assumptions are right versus wrong. They will be wrong a lot more often. There

is nothing more irritating than a person who has "their truth" which is nothing more than a dramatic invention. It is hard to keep up with someone who defines reality by their inventions without an attempt to discover the truth.

9. **"Seek first to understand**, then to be understood."

10. **Challenge yourself.** Jon Krakauer wrote, "And I also know how important it is in life not necessarily to be strong but to feel strong, to measure yourself at least once, to find yourself at least once in the most ancient of human conditions, facing blind, deaf stone alone, with nothing to help you but your own hands and your own head."

These small shifts, when implemented, will help you keep momentum. There is a flow to the abundance, and like it or not, you are the only person who can take yourself out of the flow. With our own belief barriers, perceived limitations, and stories, we hinder the speed of Light.

These lists are not easy, but integrating just one of these ideas per week will create compounding commitment.

CHAPTER 5

explore

I am grateful for religion. Religion, when practiced well, can provide a lot of love, stability, groundedness, and unexpected blessings. Religion provided me structure, boundaries, community, and deliverance when I was a danger to myself.

That is why I called religion a bridge. I was on one side of a chasm. I could see the other side, and I knew *There* is where I wanted to be. With the help of grace and forgiveness, I was able to climb out from rock bottom. Religion, along with Christ, helped me develop myself into a habitable vessel for the Holy Spirit. Religion helped me make the house that Christ indwells.

Eventually, we cross the bridge.

We get to a point where we are not finished growing, but God calls us away from the bridge, away from religiosity.

We may not leave, however. There are many who fail to launch. Many make their home under the bridge and become trolls of Christianity. Their savior is not Christ. Their savior is their religion. They are one great act of courage away from moving out from underneath the bridge. Unfortunately, the culture of the trolls is not Christlike. It's one of fear, anger, desire, shame, guilt, and apathy. Unfortunately, these "Christians" are often the nearest to the people on the other side, the ones who desperately long to enter the Kingdom. Despite their best efforts, those trolls do more harm than good. Having *Collide-o-scopes* discolored with darkness, they are unable to share the truth about our Lord and Savior. Instead, they project onto others what they are themselves infused with. They feel good when they glorify the god they know, but their feelings of goodness come from the enemy, not the Lord. They experience pride and elitism, which feels good in comparison to lesser states like guilt and shame, but it is definitely NOT from the power of the Lord.

Please, for the love of God, explore.

Exploring means leaving behind some of the boundaries that provide security and safety. Trust in the solidity of your relationship with Christ. Maintain an acute awareness of your humanness at all times, however, and know that by yourself you are feeble and incapable.

You can fall into a chasm from both sides. Just because you entered the Kingdom once does not mean you can relax. The enemy is a feverish recruiter.

No matter where you are now, know this: You belong in the kingdom, doing what God has made you to love. You deserve a real relationship with God that makes sense for you two. You deserve to be unapologetic, unashamed, guilt-free, and fearless. You deserve to explore, to discover, and to fully be *yourself.*

Note: *being yourself* is not digging your heels into your mind-identifications. The more we relinquish control; the more we surrender to our highest intuition; the more we observe; let go of negative thoughts; love; serve; and seek a relationship with Power; the more a different *You* is magnified. You will love being *You,* because it is everything you were designed to be.

There is no danger in self-discovery. Sure, there are things to be wary of, but they do not endanger you. Often, Self is right on the other side of courage.

On the route from Here to There, you will not like everything that you discover about yourself. Fortunately, nothing you find is permanent. Unfortunately, the things about yourself that you do not like will remain until you find them. What you resist persists, until you allow yourself to return to discovery. Discover how you can take what you have allowed to define you, and then go create something new.

Discover the *You* of your dreams. The things that you love are not random. They are keys to unlocking your purpose. *Make note of what you are attracted to.* These are your breadcrumbs home.

a lesson in persistence

Once upon a time...

Two grown men asked my dad to teach them how to rollerblade. For years, my dad and his coworkers would have mush-man competitions - running, biking, rollerblading races around our local metropark. Two new employees wanted to join in the tradition, only they did not know how to rollerblade.

They said to my dad, "Find a nice, flat area of the park for us to learn."

That's easy, my dad thought. He brought them to the first parking lot, which serviced a section of the trail along the lake. For two miles, it stayed at lake level. The only trouble, my dad realized, was right next to the parking lot was one small hill that was so small that it had not registered as a hill in his memory. It was no more than a ten foot drop spread out over a hundred feet. Barely a hill. If his pupils could make it past this not-a-hill, they would be able to learn along the flat, beautiful, lakeside trail.

Both men panicked on the "hill". One of them veered off into the mud. His wheels got stuck, he twisted awkwardly, and he broke his leg. My dad helped him out of his rollerblades, into the car, to the hospital.

Several months later, once the broken leg had healed, one of the two men went out rollerblading again. Was it the man with the broken leg? Or was it the other man? How strongly had each of them committed to discovering how to rollerblade? Or after the incident, had rollerblading been firmly defined as too dangerous?

Would you try again if you broke your leg?

Would you try again if you watched someone break their leg?

In the end, the man who broke his leg gave it another go. Not to be outmatched by fear.

Fear is the mindkiller.

Doubt is the dreamkiller.

Definition is the discovery-killer. Once we make up our minds about a person, a place, an activity, a thing, we stop discovering the newness about it.

I was recently camping with a couple friends. One of them was sitting around the fire looking up into the sky. She pointed at a neat line of three stars in a row, then two equidistant stars off to the right, and two more equidistant stars off to the left. "The three are the body, and the four on the outsides are wingtips. *That's my butterfly!*" she said.

I gazed up at her butterfly. I had to choke down the impulse to say, "No, that's Orion. That's his belt, that's his dog..." Thankfully I kept this information to myself.

I realized in this moment that the Greeks were no more right than my friend is. Everyone has their own perspective. Where one person sees a hunter, another person sees a butterfly. I have been seeing Orion since whoever taught me about constellations pointed him out.

My friend has inspired me to see things differently. Perhaps I will get to know the sky my own way, to return to a sense of discovery.

When I was in Tulum in the summer of 2021, I wrote:

I watched the ocean this morning.

It lapped at the shore gently. The sun glinted off the surface. Seaweed had washed ashore, a few fish, a jelly, a sargasso bulb, a scrap of a buoy, some polished glass and some smooth porcelain.

I looked out at the shimmering surface and saw beneath to great depths. The shimmering caught my eye, but I was captured by the mystery of where these things had come. Of how we were unexpectedly sharing a quiet moment in slow regard of life.

I left determined to see beneath the shimmer. I look at a crying baby and see a loving mother. I look at a muddy puddle and I see a bird bath. I look at a late bus and I see an opportunity to connect with my fellow passengers. I look at a man on the street and I see myself.

We are all here, washed ashore from great depths, ourselves great depths.

A trusting heart does not obsess over defining things. A trusting heart is curious about what God is up to. Just because life is not aligned with your preferences, or someone's perspective is different from yours, or someone's feelings are not perfectly logical, they are not wrong. Allow the contrast that arises between life and preference to ignite a sense of curiosity. "Well, this is interesting, God. To what unexpected place are you leading me?"

My friend Gabe told me, "Planning is essential, but plans are irrelevant."

Life twists and turns. Life is full of paradoxes. Things are not what they seem. Instead of making snap judgements, suspend judgment altogether. Suspend what you know into animation, and try a day knowing nothing. Blast your heart fully open with love and trust. Be here, now. Submerse yourself so deeply in the present that the concept of a detour no longer makes sense.

courage brings you closer

If your destination is Heaven and your heart is open, you are right on track.

The spiritual Path will not be laid out in neat, material, paving-stones. It will be decorated by bright crystals, in forms of beauty, love, joy, bliss, and unity. Quite often, when we are standing at a junction between force and power, when we are deciding between something worldly and something godly, we will be called to walk the direction that takes courage.

Courage will lead to trust. Trust will fill you with neutrality, a detached and knowing sensation on the brink of surrender. When you find blessings flowing to your surrendered self, hope blossoms. With hope you arrive in a relaxed place where your past feels purposeful for it has led you well. Forgiveness is available to the steward of hope. When you give and receive it, you will enter into a world of understanding. Love and compassion are the skin of understanding. They grow together. Soon, you can look upon all the faces of the world with serenity, seeing a completeness to a joyful picture. All the while, the image of God is shifting within you. It is not God who is changing, but you, so eventually you see His perfection, you experience His peace, and you are enveloped in accepting bliss exactly as you are. The illumination here is ineffable. This is enlightenment.

Enlightenment awaits the devotee to the Path, the one who is courageous enough to walk uncommonly, who constantly assesses their footsteps asking, *What Path am I on?*

This is the walk of the *Detourist.*

the road to permanence part 4/4

Apenimon was flustered. He was talking on the phone to his girlfriend, letting off some steam. "It's just…a lot. I have to take the dog for a walk, go to the post office, go to the gym, cook dinner, shower, and read a few chapters of my book for a meeting with the executives tomorrow."

"I know, hon," she said affectionately. She knew something of being overly busy as a single mom with three children.

"I'm sorry for dropping all my stress onto you," Apenimon said.

"You do not add stress to our lives, baby," she assured him. "We are blessed by you. Julio loves his new bike, by the way. And I am grateful to not have to worry about him getting hit by a car on his way to school. You do so much for everyone."

"Thank you for saying that."

"I have an idea for you," his girlfriend said. "You remember that trail that you pointed out downtown? The one that goes down into the granite quarry?"

Apenimon nodded and said, "Yea, I know the one."

"It's right by the post office. Why don't you drop your packages and go for a hike with the dog? That's three things on your list in one trip."

Apenimon loved that idea. As soon as he hung up the phone with his girlfriend, who was the mother of the boy for whom he had purchased the new bicycle, he headed out.

The trail spiraled down along the old quarry treating Apenimon to great views of the hill country. It had been rainy lately, so little rivulets hustled down the rocky trail to the river below. In a few places, the pooling waters cascaded off quarry cliffs into the lake below. In addition to the sun on his face, the man relished in the misty spray that cooled him. His dog, Piku, enjoyed himself, as well.

At the bottom of the trail, the rocky boulder field flattened into a lakeside prairie. The rain had enlivened the land, and flowers, butterflies, bees, dragonflies, birds, and other wildlife had come out in numbers. He noticed that some of the bushes had bright blue bulbs, and upon further inspection he saw that the bulbs were berries. *Blueberries!* For the next twenty minutes, he gorged himself on fruit until Piku and Apenimon arrived at a waterfall.

The sun was beginning to set but the heat of the summer day had not subsided, so the native man stripped off his clothes and plunged into the natural pool.

While Piku hunted fish along the shoreline, Apenimon decompressed in the shallow waters. The sound of the falls drowned out the world. After a while, his stress seeped out of him. For the first time in years, he truly relaxed.

He was proud of his decisions over the last year, but he realized that up until recently, he had not allowed anything to be easy. Even though he often made the right decisions, he was battling himself. The shortcut was always there, the outburst always on the other side of his tongue, and the anger at circumstances was as present as the gratitude. Now, lying in these waters he realized that he need not toil, worry, anger, or fret. The God who had made this waterfall in this prairie had made the world. In this moment, he finally allowed himself to fully believe.

When he got back to his car, there was a text message from his boss. "Call me when you get this," it said.

As he dialed his boss, he realized he was calling with a complete sense of calm. Usually a message like that would send his imagination in circles, but not then.

"Hey Boss!" he greeted.

"Apenimon!" his boss greeted cheerfully.

"How can I support you today, sir?"

His boss laughed. The man always seemed delightfully surprised by Apenimon. Sometimes, Apenimon found himself taking his kindness up a notch for his boss just to enjoy the boss's reaction. "This just could not wait until tomorrow. I was too excited to tell you. My wife and I have been working on something since we met you. We have been trying to decide what we wanted to do with the funds you located in that old tornado shelter."

"Oh?" Apenimon was intrigued.

"I remember a while ago you said that you wished for a place where native folks, like yourself, could share your history, your outlook, your culture. We figured such a venue would do wonders for the community, be that our city is about a quarter native, and despite the years and progress, we still…well, you know, have a long way to go."

"I am liking what I'm hearing, boss."

"I didn't assign you to this project because I wanted to surprise you, but you know the build over on Maple Street? By the park?"

Apenimon was familiar and he told his boss as much. That project had been highly desirable and had gone to one of Apenimon's immediate colleagues.

"We'll it's finished now. There is going to be a ribbon cutting this Friday and we would like you to be the one holding the big scissors."

"Me, sir?!" Apenimon said, aghast.

"Well, it only makes sense. You see, the center is called The Apenimon Culture Park. Seeing as I don't know any other Apenimons…"

"It would be an honor, sir," Apenimon said. When he hung up the phone, he dried the tears in his eyes. *God is so good*, he thought.

Resources

APPENDIX A: GENESIS

1 In the beginning God created the heaven and the earth.

2 And the earth was without form, and void; and darkness was upon the face of the deep. And the Spirit of God moved upon the face of the waters.

3 And God said, Let there be light: and there was light.

4 And God saw the light, that it was good: and God divided the light from the darkness.

5 And God called the light Day, and the darkness he called Night. And the evening and the morning were the first day.

6 And God said, Let there be a firmament in the midst of the waters, and let it divide the waters from the waters.

7 And God made the firmament, and divided the waters which were under the firmament from the waters which were above the firmament: and it was so.

8 And God called the firmament Heaven. And the evening and the morning were the second day.

9 And God said, Let the waters under the heaven be gathered together unto one place, and let the dry land appear: and it was so.

10 And God called the dry land Earth; and the gathering together of the waters called he Seas: and God saw that it was good.

11 And God said, Let the earth bring forth grass, the herb yielding seed, and the fruit tree yielding fruit after his kind, whose seed is in itself, upon the earth: and it was so.

12 And the earth brought forth grass, and herb yielding seed after his kind, and the tree yielding fruit, whose seed was in itself, after his kind: and God saw that it was good.

13 And the evening and the morning were the third day.

14 And God said, Let there be lights in the firmament of the heaven to divide the day from the night; and let them be for signs, and for seasons, and for days, and years:

15 And let them be for lights in the firmament of the heaven to give light upon the earth: and it was so.

16 And God made two great lights; the greater light to rule the day, and the lesser light to rule the night: he made the stars also.

17 And God set them in the firmament of the heaven to give light upon the earth,

18 And to rule over the day and over the night, and to divide the light from the darkness:
and God saw that it was good.

19 And the evening and the morning were the fourth day.

20 And God said, Let the waters bring forth abundantly the moving creature that hath life, and fowl that may fly above the earth in the open firmament of heaven.

21 And God created great whales, and every living creature that moveth, which the waters brought forth abundantly, after their kind, and every winged fowl after his kind: and God saw that it was good.

22 And God blessed them, saying, Be fruitful, and multiply, and fill the waters in the seas, and let fowl multiply in the earth.

23 And the evening and the morning were the fifth day.
24 And God said, Let the earth bring forth the living creature after his kind, cattle, and creeping thing, and beast of the earth after his kind: and it was so.

25 And God made the beast of the earth after his kind, and cattle after their kind, and every thing that creepeth upon the earth after his kind: and God saw that it was good.

26 And God said, Let us make man in our image, after our likeness: and let them have dominion over the fish of the sea, and over the fowl of the air, and over the cattle, and over all the earth, and over every creeping thing that creepeth upon the earth.

27 So God created man in his own image, in the image of God He created them; male and female He created them.

28 And God blessed them, and God said unto them, Be fruitful, and multiply, and replenish the earth, and subdue it: and have dominion over the fish of the sea, and over the fowl of the air, and over every living thing that moveth upon the earth.

29 And God said, Behold, I have given you every herb bearing seed, which is upon the face of all the earth, and every tree, in the which is the fruit of a tree yielding seed; to you it shall be for meat.

30 And to every beast of the earth, and to every fowl of the air, and to every thing that creepeth upon the earth, wherein there is life, I have given every green herb for meat: and it was so.

31 And God saw every thing that he had made, and, behold, it was very good. And the evening and the morning were the sixth day.

APPENDIX B: SERMON ON THE MOUNT

Salt and Light

13 "You are the salt of the earth. But if the salt loses its saltiness, how can it be made salty again? It is no longer good for anything, except to be thrown out and trampled underfoot.

14 "You are the light of the world. A town built on a hill cannot be hidden. **15** Neither do people light a lamp and put it under a bowl. Instead they put it on its stand, and it gives light to everyone in the house. **16** In the same way, let your light shine before others, that they may see your good deeds and glorify your Father in heaven.

The Fulfillment of the Law

17 "Do not think that I have come to abolish the Law or the Prophets; I have not come to abolish them but to fulfill them. **18** For truly I tell you, until heaven and earth disappear, not the smallest letter, not the least stroke of a pen, will by any means disappear from the Law until everything is accomplished. **19** Therefore anyone who sets aside one of the least of these commands and teaches others accordingly will be called least in the kingdom of heaven, but whoever practices and teaches these commands will be called great in the kingdom of heaven. **20** For I tell you that unless your righteousness surpasses that of the Pharisees and the teachers of the law, you will certainly not enter the kingdom of heaven.

Murder

21 "You have heard that it was said to the people long ago, 'You shall not murder, and anyone who murders will be subject to judgment.' **22** But I tell you that anyone who is angry with a brother or sister will be subject to judgment. Again, anyone who says to a brother or sister, 'Raca,' is answerable to the court. And anyone who says, 'You fool!' will be in danger of the fire of hell.

23 "Therefore, if you are offering your gift at the altar and there remember that your brother or sister has something against you, **24** leave your gift there in front of the altar. First go and be reconciled to them; then come and offer your gift.

25 "Settle matters quickly with your adversary who is taking you to court. Do it while you are still together on the way, or your adversary may hand you over to the judge, and the judge may hand you over to the officer, and you may be thrown into prison. 26 Truly I tell you, you will not get out until you have paid the last penny.

Adultery

27 "You have heard that it was said, 'You shall not commit adultery.' 28 But I tell you that anyone who looks at another lustfully has already committed adultery with them in their heart. 29 If your right eye causes you to stumble, gouge it out and throw it away. It is better for you to lose one part of your body than for your whole body to be thrown into hell. 30 And if your right hand causes you to stumble, cut it off and throw it away. It is better for you to lose one part of your body than for your whole body to go into hell.

Divorce

31 "It has been said, 'Anyone who divorces must present a certificate of divorce.' 32 But I tell you that anyone who divorces, except for sexual immorality, makes them the victim of adultery, and anyone who marries a divorcee commits adultery.

Oaths

33 "Again, you have heard that it was said to the people long ago, 'Do not break your oath, but fulfill to the Lord the vows you have made.' 34 But I tell you, do not swear an oath at all: either by heaven, for it is God's throne; 35 or by the earth, for it is his footstool; or by Jerusalem, for it is the city of the Great King. 36 And do not swear by your head, for you cannot make even one hair white or black. 37 All you need to say is simply 'Yes' or 'No'; anything beyond this comes from the evil one.

Eye for Eye

38 "You have heard that it was said, 'Eye for eye, and tooth for tooth.' 39 But I tell you, do not resist an evil person. If anyone slaps you on the right cheek, turn to them the other cheek also. 40 And if anyone wants to sue you and take your shirt, hand over your coat as well. 41 If anyone forces you to go one mile, go with them two miles. 42 Give to the one who asks you, and do not turn away from the one who wants to borrow from you.

Love for Enemies

43 "You have heard that it was said, 'Love your neighbor and hate your enemy.' 44 But I tell you, love your enemies and pray for those who persecute you, 45 that you may be children of your Father in heaven. He causes his sun to rise on the evil and the good, and sends rain on the righteous and the unrighteous. 46 If you love those who love you, what reward will you get? Are not even the tax collectors doing that? 47 And if you greet only your own people, what are you doing more than others? Do not even pagans do that? 48 Be perfect, therefore, as your heavenly Father is perfect.

Giving to the Needy

6 "Be careful not to practice your righteousness in front of others to be seen by them. If you do, you will have no reward from your Father in heaven.

2 "So when you give to the needy, do not announce it with trumpets, as the hypocrites do in the synagogues and on the streets, to be honored by others. Truly I tell you, they have received their reward in full. 3 But when you give to the needy, do not let your left hand know what your right hand is doing, 4 so that your giving may be in secret. Then your Father, who sees what is done in secret, will reward you.

Prayer

5 "And when you pray, do not be like the hypocrites, for they love to pray standing in the synagogues and on the street corners to be seen by others. Truly I tell you, they have received their reward in full. 6 But when you pray, go into your room, close the door and pray to your Father, who is unseen. Then your Father, who sees what is done in secret, will reward you. 7 And when you pray, do not keep on babbling like pagans, for they think they will be heard because of their many words. 8 Do not be like them, for your Father knows what you need before you ask him.

9 "This, then, is how you should pray:
'Our Father in heaven, hallowed be your name, 10 your kingdom come, your will be done, on earth as it is in heaven. 11 Give us today our daily bread. 12 And forgive us our debts, as we also have forgiven our debtors. 13 And lead us not into temptation, but deliver us from the evil one.'

14 For if you forgive other people when they sin against you, your heavenly Father will also forgive you. 15 But if you do not forgive others their sins, your Father will not forgive your sins.

Fasting

16 "When you fast, do not look somber as the hypocrites do, for they disfigure their faces to show others they are fasting. Truly I tell you, they have received their reward in full.

17 But when you fast, put oil on your head and wash your face, **18** so that it will not be obvious to others that you are fasting, but only to your Father, who is unseen; and your Father, who sees what is done in secret, will reward you.

Treasures in Heaven

19 "Do not store up for yourselves treasures on earth, where moths and vermin destroy, and where thieves break in and steal. **20** But store up for yourselves treasures in heaven, where moths and vermin do not destroy, and where thieves do not break in and steal. **21** For where your treasure is, there your heart will be also.
22 "The eye is the lamp of the body. If your eyes are healthy, your whole body will be full of light. **23** But if your eyes are unhealthy, your whole body will be full of darkness. If then the light within you is darkness, how great is that darkness!

24 "No one can serve two masters. Either you will hate the one and love the other, or you will be devoted to the one and despise the other. You cannot serve both God and money.

Do Not Worry

25 "Therefore I tell you, do not worry about your life, what you will eat or drink; or about your body, what you will wear. Is not life more than food, and the body more than clothes?

26 Look at the birds of the air; they do not sow or reap or store away in barns, and yet your heavenly Father feeds them. Are you not much more valuable than they? **27** Can any one of you by worrying add a single hour to your life?

28 "And why do you worry about clothes? See how the flowers of the field grow. They do not labor or spin. **29** Yet I tell you that not even Solomon in all his splendor was dressed like one of these. **30** If that is how God clothes the grass of the field, which is here today and tomorrow is thrown into the fire, will he not much more clothe you—you of little faith? **31** So do not worry, saying, 'What shall we eat?' or 'What shall we drink?' or 'What shall we wear?' **32** For the pagans run after all these things, and your heavenly Father knows that you need them. **33** But seek first his kingdom and his righteousness, and all these things will be given to you as well. **34** Therefore do not worry about tomorrow, for tomorrow will worry about itself. Each day has enough trouble of its own.

Judging Others

7 "Do not judge, or you too will be judged. **2** For in the same way you judge others, you will be judged, and with the measure you use, it will be measured to you.

3 "Why do you look at the speck of sawdust in your brother's eye and pay no attention to the plank in your own eye? **4** How can you say to your brother, 'Let me take the speck out of your eye,' when all the time there is a plank in your own eye? **5** You hypocrite, first take the plank out of your own eye, and then you will see clearly to remove the speck from your brother's eye.

6 "Do not give dogs what is sacred; do not throw your pearls to pigs. If you do, they may trample them under their feet, and turn and tear you to pieces.

Ask, Seek, Knock

7 "Ask and it will be given to you; seek and you will find; knock and the door will be opened to you. **8** For everyone who asks receives; the one who seeks finds; and to the one who knocks, the door will be opened.

9 "Which of you, if your son asks for bread, will give him a stone? **10** Or if he asks for a fish, will give him a snake? **11** If you, then, though you are evil, know how to give good gifts to your children, how much more will your Father in heaven give good gifts to those who ask him! **12** So in everything, do to others what you would have them do to you, for this sums up the Law and the Prophets.

The Narrow and Wide Gates

13 "Enter through the narrow gate. For wide is the gate and broad is the road that leads to destruction, and many enter through it. **14** But small is the gate and narrow the road that leads to life, and only a few find it.

True and False Prophets

15 "Watch out for false prophets. They come to you in sheep's clothing, but inwardly they are ferocious wolves. **16** By their fruit you will recognize them. Do people pick grapes from thornbushes, or figs from thistles? **17** Likewise, every good tree bears good fruit, but a bad tree bears bad fruit. **18** A good tree cannot bear bad fruit, and a bad tree cannot bear good fruit. **19** Every tree that does not bear good fruit is cut down and thrown into the fire. **20** Thus, by their fruit you will recognize them.

True and False Disciples

21 "Not everyone who says to me, 'Lord, Lord,' will enter the kingdom of heaven, but only the one who does the will of my Father who is in heaven. **22** Many will say to me on that day, 'Lord, Lord, did we not prophesy in your name and in your name drive out demons and in your name perform many miracles?' **23** Then I will tell them plainly, 'I never knew you. Away from me, you evildoers!'

The Wise and Foolish Builders

24 "Therefore everyone who hears these words of mine and puts them into practice is like a wise man who built his house on the rock. **25** The rain came down, the streams rose, and the winds blew and beat against that house; yet it did not fall, because it had its foundation on the rock. **26** But everyone who hears these words of mine and does not put them into practice is like a foolish man who built his house on sand. **27** The rain came down, the streams rose, and the winds blew and beat against that house, and it fell with a great crash."

28 When Jesus had finished saying these things, the crowds were amazed at his teaching,

29 because he taught as one who had authority, and not as their teachers of the law.

Made in the USA
Las Vegas, NV
21 August 2022